THE HEALING DRAMA

THE HEALING DRAMA

PSYCHODRAMA AND DRAMATHERAPY
WITH ABUSED CHILDREN

ANNE BANNISTER

FREE ASSOCIATION BOOKS / LONDON / NEW YORK

Published in 1997 by
Free Association Books Ltd
57 Warren Street, London W1P 5PA
and 70 Washington Square South,
New York, NY 10012–1091

ISBN 1 85343 382 9 hardback; 1 85343 383 7 paperback

Impression 01 00 99 98 97   5   4   3   2   1

Produced for Free Association Books by
Chase Production Services, Chadlington, OX7 3LN
Printed in the EC by J.W. Arrowsmith, Bristol.

CONTENTS

ACKNOWLEDGEMENTS

I wish to acknowledge colleagues at the NSPCC who have taught me so much and supported me over the years, especially those who have worked with me at the Child Sexual Abuse Consultancy, including Eileen Gallagher, Carol Dey, Bobbie Print, Mai Walton, Di Grimshaw, Irene Dawson and Elaine Halliwell. Staff at the Headley Library, NSPCC London have also been most helpful.

My sons Peter and Adrian and my grandchildren Sean, Aaron, Holly and Callum have also taught me much. To my colleagues in psychodrama, especially my Trainers, Marcia Karp and Ken Sprague, I am indebted and also to psychodramatists Paul Holmes (who encouraged my writing), and John Casson, Jan Costa, Kate Kirk, Jenny Biancardi and many others who have shared information on child sexual abuse. For ideas in dramatherapy I owe much to Dorothy Langley and Ann Cattanach. Most of all, I thank my husband Stan for his support whilst writing this book.

To all the abused children, abused adults, and the parents and friends of survivors with whom I have worked, I extend my gratitude. Your generosity in sharing your triumphs and pain has enabled me to continue the work.

> If a child calls you, bring your own childhood along.
> Children are the uncrowned kings.
> We are their subjects: we hold them so they can laugh.
> A child: that is some faith.
> Give him a finger and he gives you the whole hand.
>
> from *The Book of Children*
> by J.L. Moreno (1912)

PREFACE

Throughout this book, case examples have been given to illustrate the various techniques. These are drawn from my experience of working for over twenty years with abused children. However, to preserve confidentiality the names and identities of the children have been completely changed. Sometimes I have amalgamated information from several children to illustrate one instance from a therapy session. Frequently I have changed the type of abuse, age and gender of the child and family details. However, the therapeutic moments described have all occurred either within my own practice or, occasionally, within the practice of therapists whom I supervised.

1 HOW CHILDREN COMMUNICATE

A tinkling of bells was heard, and Peter, who knew the fairy
language, of course understood it.

from *Peter Pan* by J.M. Barrie

*Annie discovered the dressing-up box during her second session in
the playroom. Very quietly, without speaking, she selected a long,
floaty red skirt which she pulled on over her jeans, and a purple
cloak which she draped round her shoulders. The cloak slipped off
and she turned to the therapist for assistance. 'Tie it please', she
whispered, in her quiet, 'little girl' voice. The therapist had already
noted that even though Annie was eight years old she spoke in the
indistinct, slightly whining voice of a timid three-year-old. Annie
rummaged in the box and eventually, with an air of 'Eureka!',
drew out a large straw hat with a wide brim. She placed it on her
head and gazed with satisfaction at her reflection in the mirror.
She turned to the therapist. 'Servant', she demanded imperiously,
'clean this room and get Betty and Hetty to help you.' She gestured
towards two rag dolls, who were sitting idly on a chair. Tenderly
she picked up a baby doll from its cot and handed it to the
therapist. 'Look after the baby as well while I am out and make
sure everyone behaves themselves.' 'Certainly, your Majesty',
replied the therapist/servant, rather ingratiatingly. 'I will care for
the baby myself.' 'Humph', snorted the Queen. 'Make sure you do
some of the cleaning too.'*

During the first session the therapist had been careful to make an
agreement with Annie to reassure her that she had some control
over the content of the sessions and over the therapist herself.
Rapport built slowly during that first week but by this second
session it was obviously good enough for Annie to decide that she
could safely communicate her feelings. Using the metaphor of the
powerful Queen, one which is common in fairy stories, Annie was
able to show the therapist that she enjoyed having some control
and power.

She had been referred for treatment because she was frequently bullied at school and she had been abused many times in her life. Her father and older brother had sexually abused her and both parents had physically neglected her. Then her father left home and a stepfather moved in. He physically abused both Annie, her younger sister and her mother. Later he sexually assaulted Annie also. She was now in foster care and very withdrawn, wetting and soiling herself often.

Annie chose the metaphor of the Queen and immediately she was able to show, just by the literal use of a strong, powerful voice, that she was worth listening to. Using the 'story', which she devised herself, she communicated to the therapist her understanding of how babies should be cared for (which was not her own experience) and later, as we shall see, she demonstrated her views on justice, families and death. She was also able to show her anger in an acceptable way. The unacceptable bedwetting and soiling ceased and relationships with other children improved.

COMMUNICATING THROUGH PSYCHODRAMA

Early this century, around 1908, Jacob Levy Moreno, a medical student who was to go on to qualify as a psychiatrist, noticed children playing in the Augarten, a large park in Vienna. He studied their creativity and noted their spontaneity. Probably to the children's surprise, he joined in, taking their creations seriously and encouraging them to act out fairy stories. He realised that the children communicated easily through such games and, unlike most adults who dismissed the games as 'childplay', he saw the potential for change, not only in individual children, but in the group and within the community as a whole (Marineau 1989).

From these beginnings Moreno devised psychodrama, sociometry and group psychotherapy. He even founded a small theatre for the children in Vienna and through dramatic improvisations he worked out the theory and measurement of interpersonal relationships which he called sociometry and which he later used successfully in the Hudson School for Girls in New York. In the early 1930s, in America, where he was now living, Moreno carried out research and presented papers in which he first used the term 'group psychotherapy'. He realised that the interactions within a group of clients or patients was just as powerful as the interaction between the therapist and the client. He coined the term 'tele' to describe positive or negative interpersonal sensitivity. He understood that tele was not only a spontaneous feeling between two individuals but was part of, and dependent on, a larger structure of family, group and community. In this he pre-dated the work of Bronfenbrenner (1979) who explained the parts culture and environment play in child development. Also, to some extent, Moreno was anticipating the theories of John Bowlby (1969) on the attachment of children to their mothers or mother figures.

Moreno's invention of psychodrama as a therapeutic method and a means of communication, particularly with children, is our focus in this book. Moreno was clear that psychodrama could be used either as group psychotherapy or with individuals (Moreno 1965). He describes three basic psychodrama techniques which he links with the stages of child development (Fox 1987). Stage 1 is the period when babies discover that they have a separate identity and this stage compares with the psychodramatic technique of 'the double' or 'doubling'. Stage 2 is the time when infants recognise 'the self' and this compares with the technique of 'the mirror' or 'mirroring'. Stage 3 is the stage of recognition of the other and this links with 'role reversal' technique. These three stages have strong links with a theory of child development much used in dramatherapy and this will be discussed later.

The technique of 'doubling' is essential to psychodrama. Since psychodramatists say 'show me', instead of 'tell me', this can be illustrated using Annie as an example.

In the first therapy session Annie found it difficult to speak. When she did so it was in a tiny, quiet voice. The therapist sat beside her and unobtrusively 'doubled' or copied her body position. She began to sense some of Annie's feelings. 'Can I pretend to be you for a minute?' she asked. Annie nodded. The therapist spoke in a very small voice. 'It's a bit scary being here. I don't know what's going to happen.' Annie smiled a little. 'Will I have to talk to her about things I don't want to?' the therapist continued, as Annie. Annie looked up, interested. The therapist moved away slightly and resumed her own body position, signalling that she had now changed roles. 'Is that worrying you Annie?' she asked. Annie nodded. 'Well, shall we make an agreement? We could write down what you would like to talk about.' Annie moved to the whiteboard on the wall. 'I'll write it on here', she said. 'How do you spell Agreement?'

Doubling is the technique whereby another group member, or the psychodrama director, says the words which the protagonist is unable to speak. It is essential that the director checks out if the double is truly speaking that which is unspoken. With children it is particularly important that doubling is not confused with mimicking which is humiliating for a child. When used carefully and sensitively with a child in a one-to-one situation I have found that it is an excellent way to show children that their communications are understood, even if they are silent. It is much more effective than an interrogation when a child is asked many questions, to which the answer is usually 'Dunno'. It is easy to see the connection which Moreno made with the first developmental stage of 'identity'. The child may be asking herself, 'Who am I and what do I feel?' Doubling can help her to clarify this.

The second technique, of 'mirroring', occurs when a child is invited to witness a situation which she has just described so that she can see it 'as if in a mirror', and experience it in a slightly more objective manner. Annie was asked to do this in a later session when she was working on the relationship with her older brother who had abused her.

'I should have thumped him', Annie said, morosely, looking down at the floor. 'Or told mum, or something ... I'm stupid.' The therapist asked her to choose a doll to be her brother and a doll to be herself. She chose a large stuffed teddy bear, about three feet high, to be her brother and a small rag doll, about a third of the size, to be herself. She placed them together and watched whilst the therapist began to re-enact the scene according to the information Annie had already given. Annie stopped the scene after a few moments. 'He was big' she said, 'there was no way I could have thumped him. And I did tell my mum, she told me not to tell lies.'

Annie had been blaming herself for her own abuse because most of the adults in her world so far had done so. Her father blamed her for 'enticing' him. She was about four years old when he first sexually abused her. Her mother told her she was a liar and her stepfather said he was hitting her because she was a bad child. She had internalised these ideas and it was necessary for her to look at the situation less subjectively to see where the responsibility lay.

Most of Annie's early work was done metaphorically and she constantly and spontaneously carried out the technique of 'role reversal' without any prompting from the therapist. She played 'the servant' roles, Betty and Hetty, interchangeably, standing behind each doll and speaking a few lines. Of course, she played 'the Queen', her favourite role, constantly, and occasionally she played a King, a wicked fellow who, unlike the Queen, had no idea of what was fair. Being fair was a concept with which Annie was very concerned, as one would expect for an eight-year-old. The technique of role reversal is used to move on the action and also to give insight into the role of 'the other' as opposed to oneself.

Adam Blatner, an American psychodramatist, has a theory of child development which builds on Moreno's ideas. In the *Art of Play* (1988) which he wrote with his wife Allee Blatner, he describes four stages, the 'dermal', the 'playful', the 'useful' and the 'co-operative'. He compares the first two stages with the oral and anal stages in analytic theory. He describes the dermal as a sensory, exploratory stage and the playful as the beginnings of interaction with other objects and people. 'Look at me', is the way he describes the useful stage – obviously the child is gaining an identity and interacting with others. The final stage of co-operation is when the child can function well in a group. He compares his last two stages with the phallic and oedipal stages of analytic theory. It will be seen that this description is similar to Moreno's explanation and also has links with the dramatherapeutic theory of development which follows.

COMMUNICATING THROUGH DRAMATHERAPY

During the 1950s, in England, Peter Slade was working with children in education, using drama. He was fascinated by the way in which children use their play as a means of educating themselves, and others. He also noted that 'natural therapy' seemed to be taking place during much of children's dramatic play (Slade 1995). He then realised that by extending this he might be able to do what he called 'conscious and intended therapy' whilst playing with children. One of his most important maxims is that we should beware of treating the 'apparent' problem and look at what the child is actually communicating to us.

His work was extended and widened by many, including Sue Jennings (1987). Jennings is particularly interested in how drama is used in development and in ritual as well as in therapy. The theory of development used in dramatherapy is not far removed from Moreno's idea of Identity, Recognition of Self and Recognition of Other. Dramatherapists call the three stages Embodiment, Projection and Role (Jennings 1995).

From birth babies explore their own bodies and their physical sensations. They are seeking their own identity. This is embodiment play. During the first year they begin to explore the immediate external world and they project feelings and intentions upon objects and people in their surroundings. This is projective play, they are finding a sense of self through their relationship with other objects. Eventually, usually in the third year, children are ready to play roles with others, to practise their own future roles and to explore the roles of others.

'I will warn you once', instructed Annie, as the Queen, 'and then it's off with your head.' She spoke firmly and clearly to a male doll whom she had apparently caught hitting Betty, one of the female dolls. 'You must not hit your wife, is that clear?' The Queen proceeded in her stately way around the room. She stopped to speak to a small boy doll. 'Are you all right?' she asked. 'I haven't done anything', Annie replied, as the boy. 'Well that's all right', the Queen replied. 'I'm a fair Queen, but any messing and it's off with your head too.'

Annie had a clear sense of justice but she needed to confirm this through play since the behaviour of many of the adults in her family was unjust. She was showing the therapist her idea of justice and the therapist confirmed this by her acceptance of the role. Occasionally Annie would take on the role of 'King Henry', an evil King who was particularly dangerous to babies. It was important for the therapist to mirror the fear which the babies felt.

Annie chose a pair of baggy trousers which she pulled on over her skirt. She pushed a plastic sword down one leg. A felt hat was pulled down firmly on her head. As the King she advanced towards twin baby dolls who were lying in the cot. He hit one with his sword. The therapist, as the baby, screamed in terror, 'Stop, stop, I'll tell mum.' The King smiled, cruelly. 'She won't do anything.' He continued to hit the crying baby, whose cries became weaker and then stopped. 'No one can hear you, and now you are dead.' The King put his sword back into the baggy trousers and strode away. The therapist, changing role to the other twin, spoke quietly. 'He has killed my twin and no one knows except me.'

The technique of exaggerating the feeling is used deliberately in psychodrama by a director who wishes a protagonist to re-experience fully the emotions of a past event. It is used naturally in dramatherapy when working within a fairy-story metaphor. Annie was able to change an abuser into a killer and a child who was 'scared to death' into a dead child because in fairy stories these things are frequent. I have written more fully elsewhere about the theme of the 'dead baby' (in Jennings 1995). Children frequently bring a dead baby into their play and it seems to be a metaphor to represent their feelings when they are trying to show extreme trauma which they have suffered. Young children often use the phrase 'He's just a little bit dead', showing that they have not fully conceptualised the finality of death. Of course, babies do die in families and their surviving siblings often act out the death scene and find space, within the therapy, to express their grief which they may have contained in order to protect grieving parents.

Annie, however, was probably communicating her sense that a part of her had died when she was abused. In order to cope with severe trauma we often 'shut down' feelings to lessen the pain. Abused children may feel numb. They frequently dissociate from reality at the first signs of further impending pain or abuse. Eventually this dissociation may become involuntary and so the child spends much time feeling 'out of touch'. Annie needed to grieve for the part of her that had died and, most important for her, she needed to communicate the enormity of what had happened to all her extended family who had either ignored her plight or underestimated it.

The therapist judged that in this case Annie was referring to the death of her inner child. Annie seemed to confirm this in a subsequent scene.

Annie collected all the dolls she could find in the playroom and then asked for more. She utilised plastic figures, animals and puppets. She dressed herself in the Queen's robes. 'You must all come to the funeral party for my dead baby', she announced. 'That includes you King', pointing to a large teddy bear. 'You must come, Betty, and all the children.' She pointed to various groups of dolls. 'Grandma and grandad and all the aunties and uncles and the cousins and their friends, everyone has to come. Everyone must know she is dead.' She walked around the assembly carrying the 'dead baby' in her arms. She told everyone that the King had killed her. The therapist asked where the twin baby was. 'Safe at home. She doesn't have to come because she knows.' The funeral party was much like a birthday party. Annie had been delighted to have her first experience of a birthday party recently, at her foster parents' home. When the 'party food' had all been consumed the Queen wrapped the dead baby in a colourful shawl and placed her under a large floor cushion. The therapist, who had played the role of several guests, now moved towards the surviving twin baby who lay in a cot, outside the scene. She took the role of the baby. 'I want my mummy', she said, holding the doll in front of her. The Queen moved swiftly to pick up the baby. 'It's all right', she said, 'I can look after you now.'

Throughout her work Annie was communicating with the therapist in the best way she knew, through play. The therapist was helping her to do so by utilising methods from psychodrama and from dramatherapy to enhance communication. She was not changing the action by introducing her own material, although sometimes in educative dramatherapy this is appropriate. The therapist was using what Peter Slade called 'natural therapy' and introducing some 'conscious therapy' by means of psychodrama and dramatherapy. These two methods, psychodrama and dramatherapy, were woven, seamlessly, into a whole, using whatever seemed most appropriate for the moment.

COMMUNICATING THROUGH PLAYTHERAPY

Playtherapy, as it is taught in Britain, has emerged from dramatherapy during the last twenty years, and was probably stimulated by the work of Virginia Axline (1947) and especially by her later book *Dibs: In Search of Self* (1964). Axline had been influenced by the work of Carl Rogers (1951) whose Person Centred Therapy offered a radical alternative to some of the more directive, interpretive therapies which had been popular in most of the Western world until the time of the Second World War. More recently therapists have become aware of abuses of power in gender and in race and class but one of the main abuses is still by adults to children.

As a therapist who has worked constantly with abused children and adults the Person Centred approach has been absolutely necessary for me to ensure that I did not use my power as an adult, or as a therapist, to inflict further abuse.

Ann Cattanach, who has written movingly about her playtherapy with abused children (1992), is clear that the playtherapy that she uses and teaches has its roots in dramatherapy. She also places emphasis on story writing, usually by the children themselves, although she may write a story down if the child is too young to write. She describes playtherapy for the abused child as an exploration through play which helps the child to make sense of her experiences. The role of the therapist is to help the child to use the play materials to express herself. I would add that it is important that the therapist also witnesses the child's self-expression. In other words, the play is used as a means of communication between the child and the therapist. Although I am sure that children seek to make sense of their experiences through playing alone, the therapy lies within the relationship which develops between child and therapist. This is the difference between 'just playing' and play which is purposeful and therapeutic.

For abused children this witnessing and facilitating seems to be essential. It may be that children become blocked or stuck in a stage of play because the abuse has blocked their development. The therapist then is helping to move the block so that they can proceed to the next stage. Many skilled and experienced foster parents of abused children will confirm that when children are taken into foster care they are frequently acting at much earlier levels than their chronological age would indicate. Sometimes this is masked by a veneer of learned adult behaviour. When they are allowed to be children they regress, sometimes rather distressingly, to a very early age. If the foster parent can understand this and cope with it the child can then grow and function to a level which is more suitable to his or her age in years. This rapid 'growing up' can be facilitated very well with playtherapy.

Playtherapy does tend to be a generic term which is used to describe all kinds of therapeutic work with children, from Melanie Klein's psychoanalytic playtherapy to Margaret Lowenfeld's Sand Tray therapy. It is most often used to describe work with younger children or sometimes with children who have learning difficulties.

I prefer to describe my work as 'child centred therapy' and to include techniques from art therapy and even dance movement therapy if these seem appropriate for a particular child. I use the term 'child' in a positive way and may use it in this book to describe young people of all ages, although if an adolescent felt demeaned by the term I would respect that view.

COMMUNICATING THROUGH CHILD CENTRED THERAPY

Carl Rogers insisted that client centred therapy was not a technique or tool but stemmed from a basic attitude towards people, in other words from a personal philosophy. A truly child centred philosophy can be difficult to accept if the pervasive culture stems from an attitude which sees children as possessions. A child centred approach views children as holding the power to heal themselves. It seems obvious that a therapist who holds this view will also have a deep respect for her own worth and value. Working in a child centred way reminds us constantly of the need to have worked through our own insecurities first.

A child centred approach, although permissive and non-directive, does not mean that the therapist has no boundaries. On the contrary, boundaries of behaviour, of time and place, and even of the content of the sessions, will be appropriately agreed with the child. These boundaries will be discussed specifically in chapter 4. Neither does a child centred approach entail a passivity on the part of the therapist. The child needs to feel a positive regard and an empathic understanding from the worker.

Rogers described this process in these words:

> It is the counsellor's function to assume, in so far as he is able, the internal frame of reference of the client, to perceive the world as the client sees it, to perceive the client himself as he is seen by himself, to lay aside all perceptions from the external frame of reference while doing so, and to communicate something of this empathic understanding to the client.
>
> (Rogers 1951: 29)

I have described it rather more simply as 'following the child's agenda'. (Bannister 1992). In the interactive approach which I use, the only control which the therapist uses is that of care. By taking pains to ensure agreement, by setting clear boundaries and by working within a framework, so that the session proceeds safely from the beginning through the middle and to the end, the therapist ensures that the child has space to be heard, to be witnessed and to be understood.

Alice Miller in *Banished Knowledge* (1990) quoted Stettbacher on the process of therapy. He described it in four stages:

1. Describing the situation and one's emotions

2. Experiencing and expressing emotions

3. Querying the situation

4. Articulating needs

For children to be able to experience this process it is essential that they are heard, witnessed and understood. They then may be in a position to query the situation and so to articulate their needs.

Moreno, in a well-known quotation, described the therapeutic encounter as

> a meeting of two, eye to eye, face to face. And when you are near I will tear your eyes out and place them instead of mine, and you will tear my eyes out and will place them instead of yours, then I will look at you with your eyes and you will look at me with mine.
>
> (Moreno 1977: frontispiece)

This is a dramatic way of saying what Rogers said about seeing the world as the client sees it. It is helpful to remember that children usually assume that their perception of reality is the only one. The younger the child the more strongly this idea persists. A child assumes that as she describes her reality through play and by the use of symbols or metaphor, the adult understands that reality and, indeed, has the same perception. Hence the frustration and despair when an adult fails to appreciate the child's point of view.

The technique of 'doubling', previously described does, of course, help the therapist to experience the child's reality, as well as helping the child to be heard.

Annie was using the doll's house to show two sisters playing in their bedroom. She put two girl doll figures on the bed. 'They are laughing', she said, rolling the two small figures around. She picked up a male doll figure. 'He comes in and whack!' She demonstrated graphically as the male doll thumped the two little girls. 'And they hadn't done nothing', she said indignantly. 'We girls feel this is not fair' remarked the therapist, doubling the little girls, one of whom she presumes is Annie. 'It's not fair' agreed Annie, bringing the play into reality, 'and he hits and hits and that's it.' She continued to demonstrate until she gave up, exhausted. 'And no one stops him', said the therapist, expressing the feeling of vulnerability and hopelessness which she heard in Annie's voice and in her body language.

The therapist has now confirmed the child's reality and also confirmed that Annie's response to the beating was valid. She has witnessed her pain and not tried to justify the beating as 'punishment'. She has not followed her own agenda by asking questions. It may be that a child abuse investigation needs to be pursued, especially if the child is in danger currently, and if abuse has not been disclosed before. That, however, is a matter for consideration

and consultation with a supervisor or manager. It is not a cue for
the therapist to start asking lots of investigative questions.

COMMUNICATING WITH CHILDREN WHO CANNOT PLAY

Some children are so badly damaged that they are unable to play.
It may be that their development has not progressed beyond the
first stage and since this stage, of embodiment play, tends to be
'messy' they may have been punished severely and so they have to
find other ways of communicating. Some of these children are
described as 'falsely mature', or 'fourteen going on forty'. It seems
as if their childhood has been totally lost.

*Alison was nine years old. She entered the therapy room and sat
down carefully, smoothing her dress. She glanced towards the
therapist and then cast her eyes down. She clasped and unclasped
her hands. She smiled politely as the therapist pointed out the play
materials but made no move towards any of them. The therapist
had been told that she and her siblings had been abused in many
ways by their carers, probably since birth, and that the school had
described her as having learning difficulties, although she had not
yet been properly assessed. Teachers were troubled by her lack of
communication. The therapist continued to explain to Alison that
she could do what she liked in the room, as long as she did not
hurt herself or the therapist, or destroy the equipment. Alison
looked up briefly but did not speak. She maintained her silence,
except for occasional monosyllables, until half way through the
second session. The therapist sat in comfortable silence nursing a
baby doll. 'I think she's gone to sleep', the therapist remarked,
looking at the doll. 'Good job we were so quiet.' 'Can I write on
that?' asked Alison, suddenly, pointing to the whiteboard which
was a feature of one wall. 'Of course. Use any of the three coloured pens.' Alison stood up and wrote her name, the date and the
name of the clinic which she was attending. She assumed the
authority of a teacher. 'You ask me questions', she said to the
therapist, 'And I will write the answers.'*

This child, who had appeared to have learning difficulties, had
chosen to communicate through writing. It was true that her spelling was highly original and sometimes almost illegible, nevertheless
she built up communication with the therapist and felt that she
was in control. She sometimes provided the questions too and the

therapist followed these hints about the direction of questioning and was patient in allowing plenty of time for answers to be written. Alison was demonstrating several points about the way she wanted to communicate. Firstly, she needed to have control. She ignored the questions she did not want to answer or wrote 'Dunt no' (don't know). She enjoyed explaining her spelling to the therapist, who did not correct her unless Alison asked for 'the proper spelling'. Secondly, she was able to keep the sessions at her own pace. It was sometimes painfully slow but the therapist had patience and a belief that she could build a therapeutic relationship in this way. Alison may also have been using the board as a means of not having eye contact with the therapist. Children frequently avoid eye contact when they have painful areas which they wish to discuss. By standing with her back to the room Alison managed to avoid eye contact naturally.

Alison worked in this way for several months, progressing from question and answer sessions to spontaneously writing long lists of 'good people' and 'bad people' (in her life) and 'good feelings' and 'bad feelings'. One day she drew a house, and a garden and then she moved towards the paints. 'Next time, I'm going to use them', she said. In the next session she quickly assembled all the paints but then only used the red. She squirted the poster paint messily over a large sheet of paper and took a thick brush. She did not speak as she smeared the paint all over the paper and over most of the table too. Alison had started playing so, of course, she started at the beginning, with embodiment play. Her progress was slow but sure.

Alison was also demonstrating that children cannot play unless they feel safe. Many severely abused children have felt unsafe for most of their lives. They spend their days in 'frozen watchfulness', a phrase commonly used two decades ago when Ruth and Henry Kempe first published their research on child abuse (Kempe & Kempe 1978). More recently this has been described as a symptom of Post Traumatic Stress Disorder by the American Psychiatric Association (in Wyatt & Powell 1988). The symptom, which is very common in children who have been physically and/or sexually abused over time is named as 'a numbing of responsiveness or reduced involvement in the external world indicated by diminished interest in activities, feelings of estrangement from others, and constricted affect'. This gives a clear diagnostic description of the symptom but 'frozen watchfulness' describes many children very accurately. The child needs to monitor the movements, the motivation, and the demeanour of every person around her. She is constantly anxious but this is expressed in a taut, unrelaxed stillness. A rabbit frozen in the headlights of a car is a metaphor which springs to mind. A sudden movement, a raised voice, from adults nearby, will evoke a twitching of the hands or eyelids. Such children often volunteer to care for younger children, partly because this may be a task to which they are accustomed but also because young children and babies are seen as less threatening.

Alison, in the example given previously, took pride in the care she gave to her younger sister, Beattie, aged five. Although the girls were now in foster care, and safe from their original abusers, Alison was extremely protective, and sometimes very bossy, towards her sister. She also resented the authority of the foster mother and, of course, this caused problems in their placement.

Beattie had, of course, also been abused for most of her young life. She spent the first six sessions of her therapy hidden under a pile of bean bags in a corner of the room. The therapist did not pressure or coax her. Beattie also had severe speech problems, a condition which appears to be fairly common in young children who have been consistently abused. Beattie soiled herself each time she came, even though the sessions lasted only twenty minutes. The therapist doubled Beattie though Beattie could probably not see her out of the pile of bags. 'I'm Beattie and I think it feels scary coming here. I don't know Diane (the therapist) very well. I'll stay in here until I feel better.'

Soon it became apparent that Beattie was watching the therapist, through a peephole between the bean bags. The therapist continued to provide a running commentary of her own activities and thoughts and occasionally tried to double Beattie in order to communicate to her that she was aware of her presence and of some of her feelings. Six short, rather smelly sessions later, Beattie emerged from the bags. Like her sister she chose the paints to express her feelings. The girls, of course, communicated with each other between sessions and it is likely that Alison had told Beattie about the paints. They were seen separately, by different therapists. The work with Alison commenced before the work with Beattie, so Alison had already commenced her brushwork with the red paint before Beattie felt able to come out from her safe place.

*Beattie staggered towards the box of poster paints, each colour in a
plastic 'squirty' container, something like a detergent bottle. She
looked like a two-year-old taking her first steps. This week she had
not soiled herself. The therapist took a very large sheet of paper
and placed it on the floor. Beattie picked up the black paint container. She squirted it almost at random. A good deal of it hit the
paper. She had not spoken during the previous sessions except to
say 'no' occasionally. 'Beattie like it', she said, smearing the paint
in the same way that her foster mother had described her smearing
faeces in their home.*

Of course, Beattie needed much more work, not only with the
psychotherapist but with a speech therapist and other professionals,
as well as her foster mother, before her development became more
equal to her chronological age. But the session marked the end of
her soiling problems and the beginning of messy embodiment play
which was more acceptable to her foster mother who, subsequently,
helped Beattie to move on to play with flour and water playdough.

COMMUNICATING – INNER CHILD TO CHILD

Children begin to communicate, of course, from their very first cry.
Donald Winnicott (1964) stated that babies are expressing their
feelings through their crying, especially feelings of satisfaction,
pain, rage and grief. It is essential for human beings to communicate with others, in order to fully experience themselves, and a
child knows this instinctively. Of course, crying is also good exercise for the limbs and lungs and most healthy children cry for
some part of every day. Sometimes this is thwarted by a mother
who cannot bear to hear the crying so she comforts the child or
pushes a 'comforter' into his mouth. Maybe the crying reminds the
mother too readily of her own feelings of abandonment or grief as
a child, or of her own feelings of pain and rage. Crying to express
satisfaction is often not acknowledged but Winnicott recognised
that a baby (and an adult) can get satisfaction by performing any
bodily functions. Adults whose voices have not been heard gain
great satisfaction in shouting or singing or both.

Although the voice appears to be a primary instrument for
communication it is certainly not the only one, as every parent
knows. Often the youngest child in a family is very late in speaking, simply because she does not need to. Her siblings, and sometimes her parents (who have become experts by this time, having

practised on the older children), anticipate her every need. She cries, she shouts, she points to objects she needs. Sometimes she does not even do that. Her brothers and sisters empathise closely, because they can remember their own needs at that age, not so long ago, and they provide the reassurance or encouragement which the child requires.

It is this empathic skill which must be acquired by the therapist working with children. Whatever the age of the therapist she must be in touch with her own inner child. This is, perhaps, the most important factor in working with children. Sometimes it seems that those who work most successfully with children have a quality of being 'childlike' which is impossible to acquire by those who feel they have lost it, or never had it. In some of the greatest workers in this area – Winnicott, Slade, and Virginia Axline, for example – this quality is expressed clearly in their writing. In others I believe it is the expression of spontaneity and creativity which most communicates the 'childlike' quality. This is something which can be practised and even be learned or at least recovered.

Moreno, in his work, talked about 'practising spontaneity'. This sounds like a contradiction. But acting spontaneously does not necessarily mean acting without thought. He pointed out that psychodramatists practise spontaneity when they play roles or double or mirror in psychodrama. To act spontaneously is to use all our senses and to trust them. It entails striking a balance between structure and chaos. It is a recipe for mental health. Children who have been abused may feel that life is full of chaos and they often complain that they need to 'sort out the muddles'. Sometimes severe structure has been imposed upon them or they have self-imposed rigid structures as a means of coping.

Those who wish to work with children need to practise their spontaneity. They can do this simply by learning how to use a creative therapy such as the ones we have been discussing, or music therapy, art therapy or dance movement therapy, for instance.

For those trained in a different way it is necessary for the therapist to be in touch with creativity. Those who can express themselves in music, art, dance, drama and so on will have an advantage but, again, this can be practised. It is unnecessary to have special talent or skills in these areas. In fact it is important to forget adult judgements about being no good at art, or drama or being 'tone deaf' (whatever that means) and having the confidence to know that all art is the expression of the artist. A 'good' artist communicates well, or gives a message which many want to hear.

A painting, a performance, a book can speak to many people, or a few. It is an expression of the artist. The therapist uses creativity and spontaneity and is in touch with all the senses, just as a baby is in touch with all the senses in its effort to learn how to communicate. The empathy of a baby is often noted by child carers. The baby knows if mother is afraid, or angry, even if she thinks she is concealing it well. Perhaps the baby uses touch, temperature, the expression in the eyes, or all of these. The tone of voice is obviously important, the smoothness or clumsiness of movements. These must all be noted by the empathic therapist.

Children are not simply small adults. Abused children whose voices have not been heard will communicate by other means. If they are unable to play they will show their pain by their actions, as Beattie did. They will copy the format used by someone they trust, such as a teacher, like Alison did. They will find a way if the listener is patient enough to wait and is creative enough to understand and accept the mode of communication which the child is using. There are as many ways for children to communicate as there are ways for therapists to work with them. Understanding the development of each particular child, and knowing that each is unique, is a first step in communicating.

An understanding of children's development, both physical and psychological, is important for therapists, whether they are working with adults or children. If they are involved in assessment of children, either for the courts or for childcare agencies, it is essential.

A useful tool for anyone who wishes to communicate with children is 'Turning Points: A Resource Pack for Communicating with Children'. It is published by NSPCC and Chailey Heritage and is inclusive to all children (NSPCC 1997).

In the next chapter we will look at several theories of child development and, in particular, at how a knowledge of these can help to make a good assessment.

2 CHILD DEVELOPMENT AND ASSESSMENT

'Do you know who made you?'
'Nobody, as I knows on,' said the child, with a short laugh ...
'I 'spect I grow'd.'

from *Uncle Tom's Cabin* by Harriet Beecher Stowe

Winnicott (1964) reminds us that defining normality in a child is not only difficult, but probably not very desirable either. When new mothers take their babies to the health clinic they want to know if they are heavier or lighter, taller or shorter than children of a similar age. They want to know when to expect their child to walk or talk and what is the deadline for toilet training. They will have received much conflicting advice. Their mothers may have advised them of expectations according to the child 'expert' who was fashionable in their day. Neighbours and friends, especially if they live in a multi-cultural area, will have different norms. They come to the clinic to hear what the professionals have to say.

The doctors and nurses at the clinic are likely to be just as confusing, their influences being just as dependent on their age, culture and training as anyone else's. However, a competent child therapist needs to have an overview of research on physical development as well as the cognitive, social and emotional development of the child. A paediatrician may have given a diagnosis of 'failure to thrive' on a particular child. Such a child may have a low body weight which increased considerably during a short stay in hospital, for instance. The educational psychologist may have discovered cognitive difficulties in this particular child. The child therapist may be asked to assess the child specifically with regard to social and emotional development or as part of a wider assessment concerning child protection.

ASSESSMENT

In making a therapeutic assessment of a child there are at least four areas which I feel should be covered. These are:

1. The child's developmental level (especially play development). This part of the assessment can be complemented by reports from the educational psychologist, teachers, the paediatrician, the GP etc.

2. The attachment or bonding of the child to parents or carers. This too can be supplemented by direct observations of child and carers together or by reports from social workers.

3. The child's coping mechanisms. Parents, foster parents or adoptive parents can provide helpful information here on how the child copes with life events and how restricted the child is in the number of ways in which he/she copes.

4. The child's emotional and therapeutic needs at present. This is the area which the child therapist needs to work on specifically.

In this chapter I will address these four areas, as I do in my own work, in an attempt to build a comprehensive picture of a referred child.

1. Child development

The therapist, depending upon his or her own training, may know the work of Mary Sheridan (1973) on children's developmental progress or the work of Arnold Gessell (1971 and 1977) on cognitive norms in children. They both focus on white, middle-class children but do provide a baseline for understanding physical and cognitive development.

However, neither Sheridan nor Gessell takes any account of the environment, particularly different cultures and classes. It is vital for workers to use their own observations of children to formulate standards of developmental levels which fit more easily into the cultures in which they work. A handbook published by the National Children's Bureau (Lindon 1993) may be helpful as a place to start.

Urie Bronfenbrenner, an American psychologist, has proposed a much more ecological way of looking at children's development (Bronfenbrenner 1979). He suggests that children's development is influenced by a series of systems which fit inside each other much like the Russian dolls which I use sometimes in my work with children. The smallest doll contains the microsystems which affect

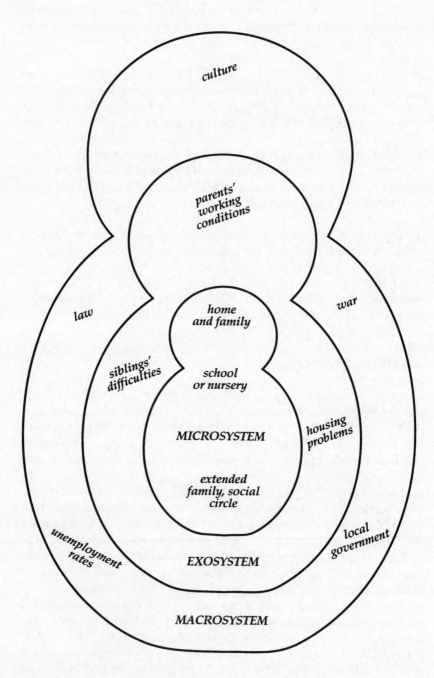

Figure 2.1 Bronfenbrenner's theory

the child directly: the home and family, the school or nursery, and maybe the extended family, church or social circle. These microsystems form links with each other, creating a mesosystem which provides the primary influences on the growth of the child.

The second 'Russian doll' contains the exosystem, that is those systems which do not directly affect the child but may affect parents (such as their working conditions), and which will have an indirect influence on the child. For instance, if a child has a sibling with learning difficulties, the decision which the parents take about education for the child with disability will affect all the siblings and may well affect their development. Similarly, housing difficulties, to which the child may be oblivious, may have a great effect on the parents or an older sibling.

The third doll represents the macrosystem or the outside influences of culture, law, unemployment and so on. Obviously a refugee child or a child in a war-torn country will be highly affected by their experiences and their development will reflect this. In a less dramatic way decisions which are made at local government level, to house all 'problem families' in high-rise flats on the outskirts of a city for instance, will have major developmental repercussions upon all the children of those families. (See Figure 2.1.)

Bronfenbrenner's theories, although not particularly startling, do have an effect upon child therapists as we begin to realise the many influences upon children, which will affect their ways of looking at their lives. We can also realise the importance of placing therapeutic intervention within the context of the family, school and cultural environment and recognising the limitations of each.

Making our own observations of children in their natural settings is an important part of our initial studies and of our ongoing experience if we are to develop and formulate our own theories. Jean Piaget observed his own children and many others during the course of his research (Piaget 1947). One of his observations was that infants and young children appear to be egocentric; they assume that the universe revolves around them and therefore that they are the cause of events. Most of us are aware that young children often believe that they have caused the death of a parent, or a divorce, because of their own behaviour. They are unable to see the world from any point of view other than their own. More recently, however, Bower (quoted in Smith & Cowie 1988) showed that children as young as four or five were able to empathise with others and see a different viewpoint. This fits in with the developmental theory of play (embodiment, projection and role play) which we discussed in chapter 1. A child of five can play a role and see the world from another perspective.

As I watch Tom, aged ten months, laughing as he plays 'peek-a-boo' with his mother, I realise that he understands that she has not really gone away even though she is hiding behind the chair. When he was younger he may have cried as she disappeared from view. Now he is confident that she is still around. He is gradually acquiring what Piaget called the 'object concept'.

Piaget also suggested that children learn in a series of 'operations' or evolving structures which grow from one stage to another. He called the stages of learning sensori-motor, pre-operational, concrete operational and formal operational. The last stage includes abstract reasoning and starts about the age of twelve, so this stage really describes young adulthood.

An operation or 'schema' can be illustrated by my description of observing Tom, aged ten months, who has now tired of playing peek-a-boo. He picks up a red ball (his favourite) and rolls it towards his mother, who rolls it back to him. He has already learned that one of the properties of the ball is its ability to roll. His mother then hands him a red brick, similar in size to the ball. He tries to roll it, not very successfully. Later he will learn that the brick has other properties, especially that it is possible to pile one on top of another.

It is most likely that Tom's mother or his older sibling will show him how to build a tower with bricks and then Tom will discover the fun of knocking them down. This interaction between children and others is stressed by Vygotsky (1934), a Russian whose work was little known in the West until the 1970s. He saw that the child did not acquire the tools of learning entirely alone but was dependent upon communication with others. A good teacher, for instance, will listen to the child and establish communication, introduce suitable materials to encourage the child's creativity and spontaneity and then, perhaps, make further suggestions during their interaction.

This could be a good starting point for a child therapist. Collaboration with someone who is more knowledgeable will produce good results, but only if children are given space to weave new concepts into their own learning and to draw their own conclusions. In fact, I have called my way of working with a child 'the interactive method' because it is not simply a therapist observing and possibly analysing a child's behaviour; it depends upon the therapist building on the child's actions, reacting to the child's communications and offering some new concepts and creative ideas when the child is ready.

Melanie Klein's theories about splitting, projection and projective identification (Klein 1975) help to explain the behaviour and development of an infant. The therapist, looking at emotional development, may turn to Klein's object relations theory to explain the severely stunted or damaged emotional development which may be seen in the child who has been severely abused in the first two years of life. Klein felt that a newborn baby has 'an integrated ego' but when anxious the baby will use defence mechanisms in order to cope.

Splitting. In the first place the baby uses the psychological defence of 'splitting' in order to protect 'the good' from 'the bad'. Good experiences are, for instance, being fed, feeling warm, being caressed. Bad experiences may be being slapped, feeling cold, feeling hungry or dirty. The baby cannot yet conceptualise that these experiences may emanate from the same source. Indeed the baby, while still engaged in exploratory or embodiment play, is not yet sure which is 'me' and which is 'the other'. So the split occurs, both in the baby ('me') and in 'the other'.

Projection and projective identification. This splitting leads to another psychological defence or coping mechanism, that of projection. The 'feel bad' part of the infant's ego may be projected onto available external objects, possibly the breast and eventually the mother or primary carer. However, the baby has a problem with the concept that mother is bad so at times the 'feel good' part of the baby is also projected onto the mother or other carer. The baby cannot yet integrate its own 'good' and 'bad' parts and neither can it bring together the 'good' and 'bad' of the carer. (See Figure 2.2.)

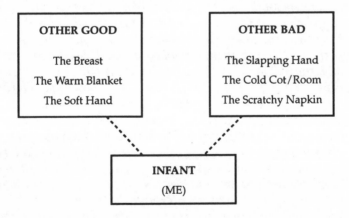

Figure 2.2 Kleinian theory

This projection onto objects is used later by the child in projective play with cuddly toys. It may be that 'teddy' is the person who holds all the 'bad thoughts' and hence 'teddy' is the one who has been naughty. Projection onto objects is also seen in the use of a 'comfort blanket' or transitional object (Winnicott 1971 & 1974). Winnicott points out that this blanket or toy may be symbolic of the breast but it is treasured by the baby for itself, and is vitally important.

Young Tom, whom we met earlier, still clings to Bluey, a rather floppy stuffed rabbit. It is a comfort to him, especially when mother is not there. It is his protector. He endows it with all kinds of good characteristics. He is omnipotent where Bluey is concerned. One day he will discard Bluey, who will fall into disuse at the bottom of the toybox.

A healthy child like Tom will integrate the good and bad parts of himself and understand that others are also unlikely to be wholly good or bad. Tom will, in a year or two, try out various roles as he plays with his friends. He can play ogres and villains, Superman or soldiers, rehearsing these roles, and integrating parts of them into his own personality as he pleases.

Developmental Stage 1 – embodiment

Alan, aged four, did not have such a happy childhood. He had been referred because he seemed unable to play. He stood awkwardly in the centre of the playroom, watching the therapist carefully. He sat down when she did. He responded when she spoke but never initiated conversation. It was known that he had been severely neglected for about the first two years of his life. He may also have been physically abused. A box of Play Doh lay open on the table between them. Idly the therapist rolled a small piece between her palms and shaped it into a ball. Alan watched intently. 'It smells funny, this stuff', she remarked, sniffing the Play Doh. Gingerly, Alan picked up a piece and sniffed it. 'I like it', he said, 'can I do it?' Over the next few weeks the therapist used Alan's capacity for embodiment play, offering him different textures such as clay (with water), finger paints and 'Slime'. She realised that he had been sensorially deprived and she brought in pieces of cloth of many colours and weaves. Smell and taste were introduced, with food-stuffs and drinks. Soon Alan was feeling the textures of fluffy toys and puppets and projecting feelings onto them. The second stage of play had begun.

It was a fairly simple task to stimulate Alan's senses and allow him to begin his own processes of exploration and healing. As he did so, of course, he experienced anger, sadness and despair. The therapist helped him to look at these strong feelings and to place them in the context of his life, both past and present.

Developmental Stage 2 – projection

Belinda was nine years old when she was referred with her older sister and younger brother. All the children had been neglected and physically abused and it was suspected that one or more of the children had been sexually abused. She was described by other professionals as being very flat, unresponsive, with learning difficulties. 'How are you today?' asked the therapist, by way of greeting in the second session. 'OK' replied Belinda. 'What's OK?' asked the therapist. Belinda shrugged. The therapist drew four circles on a whiteboard. 'These are faces', she said. 'Let's see how they are feeling.' She drew happy, sad, angry and frightened expressions on the faces. (See Figure 2.3.)

Figure 2.3 Feelings faces

Belinda looked at them blankly. She did not know what was required. Gently the therapist explained. 'This one is happy', she said. 'Why is she happy do you think?' Belinda shrugged. 'And this one is sad.' There was no response from Belinda. 'And this one is angry.' 'What's angry?' asked Belinda.

Over the next few weeks the extent of the abuse against Belinda became clear. As she had been physically and sexually abused her feelings had been denied by her abuser, who was also her father, Belinda's primary carer. Her fears had been derided, her sadness denied, her anger repressed. She was unable to know what she was feeling. She was in chaos. With the use of drawings, and later of dolls and puppets, Belinda was able first to project feelings onto other objects and eventually to own some of those feelings herself.

Developmental Stage 3 – role play

At twelve years old Charlie seemed, at first, to be like any other football-mad boy. He chatted eagerly to the therapist about the exploits of his team's stars. His foster mother had been explicit at the referral meeting. 'Charlie has been with me for three years now but sometimes I think he hasn't grown up. He is very selfish and never thinks of others. He has a terrible temper, more like a two-year-old in his tantrums. I'm dreading his adolescence.' When Charlie was about three his mother had left home and Charlie had been sexually abused by his father and father's girlfriend, and also by his uncle and aunt. In the playroom he moved around eagerly, inspecting all the equipment on offer. He played for a few minutes with clay and then drew a picture of a footballer. 'Guess who?' he asked the therapist. She had to admit her ignorance. 'I'll give you a clue', Charlie offered and took from his pocket a collection of cards, each bearing a picture of a footballer. 'It's one of them.' Charlie was skilled at drawing and the therapist immediately recognised a well-known local black football star who had been in the news recently because of racist remarks made against him by the football crowd. She spoke admiringly of his prowess and self-control. Communication was thus established between Charlie, who was black, and the therapist, who was white. Charlie talked heatedly about the racist incidents at the football ground. 'Can you be your hero for a minute and I'll be someone in the crowd?' asked the therapist. Charlie looked startled. 'I want to be like him when I grow up.' 'Well now's your chance to practise.' The football pitch was set up in the therapy room. Faces were drawn on a large whiteboard to represent the crowd. Charlie ran onto the pitch, as his hero. For a few moments he became the superhero completely. Charlie spent several sessions playing the roles of the football star, the abusive man in the crowd, the star's supporters and even the referee and the Football Association. By practising these roles he understood the effect which they had on each other. Soon he was able to move on to play roles within his own foster family and, eventually, within his family of origin.

Charlie was using role play to help him to become less egocentric, to have a perspective other than his own. He was also using psycho-drama in a very productive way to help him to experience a stage in his development which had been blocked by the traumatic events in his life from the ages of three to seven. Charlie's foster mother was pleased with his progress and reported that he was fitting into the family much better. She was still concerned, however, because she knew that he had been sexually abused and she wondered if his recent preoccupation with masturbation was a result of this. This was an opportunity for the therapist to check that the foster mother's placement worker could talk to her about what sexual behaviour can be expected in a twelve-year-old.

Sexual Development. The placement worker might have referred to the work of Sgroi (1988) or Gil & Johnson (1993) to reassure Charlie's foster mother that masturbation often begins in infancy and continues throughout childhood and adolescence. The five-year-old learns that this behaviour is not acceptable in public and usually the next few years are so full of new sensations and experiences that masturbation becomes less attractive, except perhaps at times of stress. With puberty, however, sexual feelings become stronger and so Charlie's current preoccupation was not unusual. Table 2.1 (overleaf) gives a broad indication of children's sexual development. This will be discussed more fully in chapter 6 when we look at children who sexually abuse others.

2. Attachment and bonding

In a report to the World Health Organisation in 1951 John Bowlby, who had been asked to advise on the mental health of homeless children, wrote 'What is believed to be essential for mental health is that the infant and young child should experience a warm, intimate and continuous relationship with his mother (or

Table 2.1 Children's sexual development

Pre-School 0–4	Primary School 5–10	Secondary School 11–16
Preconditions:	Preconditions:	Preconditions:
Little peer contact	Close peer contact	Separation
Random self-touching leading to masturbation.	Masturbation.	Masturbation.
	'Peeping', exposing self.	Exhibitionistic.
Curiosity about own and others bodies.	'Rude jokes'.	Touching others.
		Sexual fondling.
'Rude' language.	Sexual games.	Simulated sex.
Plays 'doctor'.	Kissing.	Intercourse.

permanent mother-substitute) in which both find satisfaction and enjoyment' (Bowlby 1951).

In many cultures throughout the world this statement would have seemed self-evident. Mothers from parts of India and Africa, native American mothers and mothers from Welsh valleys, who carried their children around on their backs, wrapped in a shawl or sari would have expressed surprise that this needed to be spelled out. In Britain, however, and many parts of the Western world, children were handed over, sometimes to a succession of nannies or nurses and sent away to school at an early age. During and before the Second World War many children were sent to strangers for their own safety. Bowlby's seminal work, *Child Care and the Growth of Love* (1953) caused radical changes in the teaching of child development, both in the medical and sociological fields.

Like Piaget, Bowlby observed children in real-life situations and in particular noted that children who had a prolonged stay in a hospital or residential nursery, with constant changes of primary carer and no constant mother or mother figure, stopped committing themselves to people and became attached only to material objects such as toys or sweets (Bowlby 1969). The children showed distress at first when carers left, but later showed no great joy or distress even when parents came or left. We must remember that at this time visiting children in hospital was extremely restricted and travel facilities for parents with children in residential nurseries were poor. In addition, parents were often discouraged from visiting their children on the grounds that 'it would upset them'.

Bowlby's work on maternal deprivation has been challenged many times since, not least by Rutter (1981). It was realised that Bowlby's interpretation was too narrow and that children could attach themselves to more than one caregiver and indeed this was beneficial to a child. Again, in many cultures such as parts of India and Pakistan and the Caribbean, this would seem obvious because children are often cared for by a constant group of extended family members, usually female. The publication of Bowlby's findings did lead to a great improvement in institutional care and foster care and also in children's hospitals. It did, however, discourage the growth of nursery care for young children and caused much anguish to working mothers in Britain.

It seems to be clear that some shared care of small children is not damaging and may well be desirable. However, the child does need to form attachments to these early caregivers and if the relationship with them is consistently warm and caring then the child is likely to be able to form subsequent relationships without too much difficulty. The child therapist needs to assess how well a child can form relationships and how well she is attached to her current and former caregivers. If a child has difficulty in forming good relationships she may need to regress to an earlier developmental stage in order to re-experience an early nurturing relationship.

Diane was eleven years old and had suffered a succession of institutional and foster placements after being removed from an abusing and neglectful family. At school she had no friends and her current foster placement was in danger of breaking down yet again because she seemed unable to form a relationship with her foster mother. On entering the therapy room for the second session she noticed a toy teaset and baby's bottle, both filled with orange juice. They had been left in the room after an earlier session with a four-year-old. 'I'm thirsty', Diane said, sitting at the table where the teatray was. 'Have some orange juice', offered the therapist. Diane poured a cup of juice from the teapot. She sipped it, looking at the feeding bottle. 'Who is that for?' she asked. 'Anybody who wants it', replied the therapist. 'For little kids?' Diane asked anxiously. 'And big ones if they want it', the therapist confirmed. The session continued with Diane writing on a whiteboard and then asking the therapist to write something also. As the therapist's back was turned Diane picked up the bottle and took a drink. This happened several times and was observed on a video camera which Diane knew was running. Eventually the therapist saw what was happening. 'Do you want some more juice in there?' she asked, since the bottle was now empty. Diane nodded.

After the session Diane told her foster mother that she had been allowed to drink from a baby's bottle. The foster mother challenged the therapist for approving such 'babyish' behaviour. This led to a helpful discussion with the foster mother and together she and the therapist formed a care plan which allowed Diane to be treated at home, for a short time daily, as a small child. She was cuddled by the foster mother and allowed to sit on her knee. She was allowed to drink juice from a bottle. Of course this plan had to be carefully explained to Diane, who agreed to it, and who understood that at other times she had to obey the 'house rules' in her foster home and in school. The foster placement was still viable and Diane seemed settled some two years later. She had made some friends and her school work was improving.

Sometimes parents will find it difficult or impossible to form relationships with their own children because of their own early deprivation. This may leave a child yearning for a closeness which cannot now be easily found. Such a child will be extremely vulnerable to child sex abusers who will recognise and seek out such children.

Edward, aged nine, had been sexually abused by a convicted paedophile for two years. Another boy, who was also being abused, had disclosed details of the 'paedophile ring' and this had led to the man's arrest. Edward had been identified as one of the man's victims and had admitted this but he had not previously disclosed anything. His mother, with whom he lived, seemed to be blaming Edward, whose behaviour had been 'difficult' for some years. Edward's mother had been taken into care herself at an early age and Edward's father had never acknowledged him. In the session Edward played with a yellow bear puppet. He instructed the therapist to pick up a brown monkey puppet. 'He wants to have his hair combed and all the bits smoothed out', he said. The monkey puppet groomed the bear puppet carefully for several minutes. 'My mum used to comb my hair when I was little', said Edward wistfully. He began to talk about his mother. The only closeness he remembered was the occasional hair combing.

It became clear that although Edward had formed an attachment to his mother this was dysfunctional in that he felt totally responsible for her. He, in fact, was parenting her and had done so for many years. He was easy prey for an abusive man who gave him 'cuddles' and who also sexually abused him. Although Edward appeared to benefit a little from some subsequent therapy, in a caring, non-abusive relationship with his therapist, he and his mother were locked in an unhappy pairing which left them both vulnerable.

This kind of attachment is not unusual, indeed throughout the years of work with abused children, I have seen many examples of children who were closely attached to extremely physically or sexually abusing parents. The fact that there is a bond is not necessarily a reason for a child remaining with such a parent.

Forming a new attachment with a non-abusive foster parent may be a vital learning experience for a child like Edward but it is not the only answer. Edward could survive better if he had a grandparent, a neighbour, or another relative with whom he could experience a bond in which he feels nurtured and loved as the child that he is. His dysfunctional attachment to his mother may persist but Edward has another model and he may then be able to form relationships in which he is not exploited. Unfortunately the 'Edwards' of the world are likely to become isolated and unable to find a more healthy attachment figure.

For more information on assessing attachment I recommend a booklet by psychotherapist Vera Fahlberg (1981).

3. Coping mechanisms

At the beginning of this chapter, when we looked at Melanie Klein's theories, we discussed 'splitting' and 'projection', both of which are psychological mechanisms for coping with anxiety or stress and which occur naturally in infants. As children grow older they usually begin to integrate their personality and only use these mechanisms occasionally at times of stress. Adults usually use more mature mechanisms such as repression, sublimation and displacement (Holmes 1992: 118).

Adults, especially disturbed adults, tend to use one or two associated coping mechanisms to alleviate anxiety-provoking situations. Children who are abused seem to use several different mechanisms and eventually these lead to coping behaviours which become fairly fixed and often cause further difficulties for the child. In my experience abused children cope with their abuse by behaving as victim or victimiser. The younger the child the more likely she is to change her behaviour frequently. She may try an extremely passive stance, keeping quiet, never crying, never complaining. She may move slightly to a 'trying to please' attitude, smiling constantly, offering to do odd jobs or errands. If she is at school the effect of both these behaviours may be that she becomes bullied. She may then move to a more aggressive stance and may bully other children. This may include stealing from children and teachers, exploiting children with threats and even physical aggression.

These behaviours lie on a spectrum from passive to aggressive and children will often move fairly quickly from one end of the spectrum to another as they try out roles which seem to fit their particular situation. Because of socialisation in many cultures, more females will use the victimised responses whereas males will be more inclined to use the victimiser behaviour but, of course, the behaviours are not gender exclusive. By the time the child reaches adolescence the behaviours may be more fixed if the child has not been able to integrate her experiences and reach a more balanced outcome.

Adolescence will, however, bring more opportunities for variations on these behaviours. The victimiser role is a very controlling one. The child seeks to control as much of her life as possible, even though she is completely unable to control the abuse which she is suffering. She may turn to drug taking as a means of controlling her own mood. She may develop eating disorders such as bulimia or anorexia as a means of controlling her body image. She may prostitute herself for financial reward as a means of controlling the manner in which she is abused. Alternatively she may develop her own victim role by running away, literally by leaving home, or by truanting from school. She may form relationships in which she is physically, sexually and emotionally abused. To keep others at bay she may neglect her personal hygiene or appearance. Her eating disorder may take the form of obesity as self-protection.

In addition many abused children will use dissociation as a coping mechanism. Of course, all children use this from time to time (as do adults). When events are painful or difficult to cope with, we may dissociate ourselves from them by 'flipping out' or 'floating away'. It is more than a 'day-dream', perhaps more akin to the feeling as anaesthesia takes hold, when the body seems separated from the mind. Perfectly normal children of five or six may convince themselves that the person who took the chocolates from mother's box was not themselves but their friend. Their friend, of course, is an imaginary one, but it helps to keep the thoughts of punishment at bay if the child imagines that the friend is going to be blamed. This is not lying as the child has convinced herself, albeit temporarily, that she was not at fault.

A child who dissociates during the abuse, in order to protect herself, may involuntarily dissociate at other times. She may therefore feel that she is separate or apart or unreal and may be unable to make relationships as a consequence. This will have an effect on self-esteem and on emotional development generally. It may lead to memory loss, where several years of life seem to have 'disappeared' from conscious memory. Sometimes children have given graphic descriptions of their abuse at a time when this has been discovered (perhaps by the disclosure of a sibling). This is recorded and much later the child presents for therapy because of behavioural difficulties.

Fiona was six when her two older sisters, aged nine and eleven, talked to their teachers about multiple sexual abuse by their father and father's friends. It was clear that Fiona was also involved and she was able to give clear statements about events, as were her sisters. There was a prosecution and conviction of several people. The girls were placed with foster parents. Four years later Fiona came to therapy because of extreme episodes of dissociation in the classroom and in her foster home. Her school work was neglected, friendships were few. She asked, after several sessions, if she could see her own statements on the abuse which she had been told that she made four years previously. She read through them with some surprise, remembering clearly only that she and her siblings were taken to a special venue (which she could describe) where the abuse occurred. Of the abuse itself, she had no memories. Gradually, over many weeks, she worked upon parts of her own statement. Firstly she acted out scenes as if it was a drama, playing the roles of her sisters and some other children, but not herself (which she asked the therapist to play). Eventually, by the use of psychodrama, and by playing the roles of her abusers (which she took spontaneously without asking the therapist), she was able to get in touch with her anger. She then, again spontaneously, reversed into her own role and there was a scene (which psychodramatists call surplus reality), which did not really happen. During this scene, which she was clear was 'what she wished had happened', she told her abusers how angry she was.

This example of Fiona's experience, which is well documented in records, shows clearly how children can completely 'forget' traumatic events and remember them (or parts of them) only when triggered by other abusive experiences or by careful exploration, together with the therapist.

In extreme cases dissociation can lead to multiple personality disorder where a child or adult will create several personalities which are split-off parts of themselves. Sometimes they are aware of these other personalities and sometimes they are not. Working with children and adults who are suffering from multiple personality disorder is becoming more frequent as practitioners are beginning to understand how the problem can be managed.

All these coping mechanisms and the overall condition of Post Traumatic Stress will be discussed further in the next chapter on 'Understanding Abuse'. During an assessment of a referred child it is important for the therapist to notice the mechanisms which the child uses naturally and to listen to parents and caregivers to hear how the child behaves in stressful circumstances. It is particularly important also, if a child is using extremely controlling behaviour, to inquire about any incidents of sexual aggression towards other children or adults. This kind of behaviour is often not reported but research shows that it is important to tackle it early on. This area of sexual aggression is further explored in chapter 6.

4. The child's therapeutic and emotional needs

Children are often referred for therapy by parents, carers or professionals, because they have assessed that the child's difficulties are caused by particular past events. Parents, especially, may ignore internal family matters which have been traumatic for the child, and fix on external events as the cause of the child's pain or behavioural difficulties.

Georgina had concerned, caring parents who felt helpless in the face of their daughter's overwhelming fear. From a confident, care-free seven-year-old she had changed into a clinging, frightened nine-year-old whose school work was suffering. A year previously she and a friend had been very upset when accosted by a 'flasher', a man committing an act of indecency in a local park. The offender, who was a local man, was eventually brought to justice after committing several other similar offences. He was given a small fine and released. Georgina was still terrified of walking the short distance from her school to home. She suffered horrific nightmares and refused to sleep without a light. If her father was away on business, which he often was, she insisted on sleeping in her mother's bed. At school her teachers were alarmed when she wrote stories about women and children who were murdered.

In a therapeutic session Georgina used toy animals to represent her family. She used an elephant for her father and told a complicated story about the elephant who wandered off into the jungle and did not come back. A huge, black spider wove a web around the remaining animals who represented her mother and sisters. She used a kangaroo as Georgina, who tried unsuccessfully to jump out of the web and to pull the others out. 'The elephant could tread on the spider and crush it', she cried excitedly, 'and tear the web to pieces with his tusks'. As soon as she had said this she looked forlorn and tearful. 'But the elephant has gone' she said, 'into the jungle'.

Both of Georgina's parents had brought her to the sessions and were seeing another therapist at the same time. The two therapists shared information. Rules about confidentiality had, of course, been carefully agreed between all the parties beforehand. The parents had told their therapist that they had temporarily separated for a few months when Georgina was seven, but they said that she was not aware of this since her father maintained frequent contact and used his business trips as an excuse not to be home more often. After receiving the information about Georgina's play, her parents' therapist advised them to talk more openly with Georgina and, in particular, her father should reassure her about his continuing love and support for her and the rest of the family.

For Georgina this was a turning point. She had, of course, realised that her parents had been estranged, but because she was not given information she was in fear of it happening again. She was still young enough to think that she had somehow caused the split. The talks with her father led to a much more open discussion with him about the sexual offender. Georgina had not been sure how much her father knew about the incident since she had previously only spoken directly to her mother on the subject. The family came back for a joint session of therapy with the two therapists.

Georgina quickly set up the toy animals again. The elephant stamped around, sometimes moving away from the family. The kangaroo hopped everywhere, into the desert and even the jungle. 'What about the spider?' asked the therapist. 'He's the one that's scared', said Georgina. 'He knows this is the elephant's family so he won't come near.'

This was a rather obvious example of a child with loving parents whose disturbed behaviour may have been exacerbated by the

sexual trauma, but who was more upset by her parents' problems
and by being kept in the dark. Trying to work with Georgina on
the sexual trauma, whilst ignoring the message she communicated
about her father, would have been unproductive. Some weeks after
this final, joint session, Georgina's mother wrote to her therapist
to say that the child seemed to be 'her old self again'.

Harry was another child who had a very protective loving
mother, but who had not been given the information he deserved.
At eleven years old he was already going around with a gang of
boys who were into petty crime. Yet Harry was a quiet child, not
achieving well at school, affectionate to his mother, but disobeying
her by truanting and running away. He enjoyed weekend trips with
his father, who was not married to his mother, but whom he saw
regularly and frequently. Both parents were very distressed when
Harry was abducted and taken away for the weekend by a man
who, it turned out, was a convicted paedophile. Harry was brought
home by the police and referred for therapy because he refused to
talk about his experience.

*In the session Harry drew a picture on the whiteboard. Several
boys were playing football. Harry said he liked football. The therapist asked what he liked best about it. 'When I score', answered
Harry, smiling. 'You must be good then, if you often score?' 'Mm',
Harry nodded. 'Anything you don't like about football?' the therapist asked, noticing some reservations in his previous answer. 'Yes',
replied Harry, looking distressed, 'when they shout black bastard if
I miss'. Harry was an attractive child with dark eyes and hair and
an olive skin. He was very like his mother in appearance. He had
previously drawn a picture of his father and told the therapist that
he was a 'big man with red hair'. The therapist asked Harry why
the boys called him such names. Harry said, 'I don't know. My
mum says it's because I'm a bit brown from being out in the sun.'
The therapist asked to see Harry's mother, Ellen, and talked to her
about herself. She found that there were family secrets about her
own mixed parentage and these had not been explained to Harry.
Talking to the therapist helped Ellen to sort out her own feelings
and she was then able to talk with Harry, with the therapist's help.
This freed Harry up and he began to draw many things that were
troubling him and he became enthusiastic about acting out scenes
using puppets. Ellen had some separate therapy of her own (with a
different therapist) and in a final joint session with Harry and his
mother the therapist was delighted to see them both using puppets
to act out family scenes.*

In fact working with Harry on his racial identity was his most pressing need. The therapist needs to decide what is most important for the child at that time. Often there are pressures to work with a child on a particular behavioural difficulty which is causing problems, either for the child or for others. In some cases, for instance, where a child is abusing others, this needs to be tackled first, if the child can accept it, because of the immediate danger, both to the child and the victims. This will be fully discussed in the chapter on sexually aggressive children. In other cases, however, it is far more productive to follow the child's agenda and work with whatever he or she presents. This gives children confidence that they are being heard.

In making an assessment, therefore, one of the key factors may be to draw up a list of areas to be tackled. This can become part of a subsequent agreement between the therapist and child regarding their sessions. It will not contain all the subjects which are eventually raised but it will build the therapeutic alliance and increase communication and understanding of the process by the child.

Writing a Report

The full report of an assessment of a child will, therefore, include the four areas which we have discussed. First, I would state some idea of the developmental level at which the child is operating, especially if this is very different from her chronological age. Some explanation of the significance of this may need to be included in the assessment so that the reader can appreciate that the therapist can work with the caregivers to progress the child's development. If this is not done then it can be erroneously concluded that the child is irremediably stuck at a certain level.

Secondly, some assessment of the child's bonding and attachment process may be given. Again, encouragement may need to be given to current carers to foster their own attachment to the child by meeting him or her at the appropriate developmental level. The therapist may also have to make it clear to the reader of the report that a dysfunctional attachment to a parent may not be allowed to continue if the child is to improve.

Thirdly, I feel that the observations and information on the child's coping mechanisms should be stated, especially where these put the child in immediate danger. For instance, a strictly controlling mechanism could lead to a child abusing others and, conversely, a child who is wholly operating at 'victim' level will be in danger of being further abused.

Lastly, the report reader needs to know what are the child's immediate emotional and therapeutic needs. If the assessing therapist is not to continue with the work it will be extremely helpful for carers and other professionals to know how to proceed with the child.

3   UNDERSTANDING ABUSE

'Why didn't you say anything?' There was pain in her voice.
'Why did you keep quiet?' but he shook his head.
extract from The Bone People, by Keri Hulme

One of the many reasons why child abuse was not recognised, or
was ignored, for so long was that children often find it difficult to
speak about it. In the extract from *The Bone People* above, the
child's friend, a woman named Kerewin, is horrified when she
accidently discovers the extent of the child's injuries which have
been inflicted by his foster father. The child has spent much time
and energy hiding the injuries out of loyalty to his abuser, whom
he also loves. This is a common story and because we adults often
do not want the responsibility which goes with the discovery of
child abuse, many of us collude with the child's denial.

*Isabel was seventeen and had been referred because she had physi-
cally abused her three-month-old baby. She described a 'happy
childhood', with middle-class parents, father a teacher and mother
a housewife. She told the therapist she had been 'a bad girl' during
her adolescence. She had tried drugs and alcohol and had an abortion at fifteen. This baby was the result of another casual sexual
encounter. In a group psychodrama session she remembered her
own early childhood and re-enacted a scene where she was crying
in her cot. She became distressed and said she was 'waiting for the
hitting'. During the 'sharing' part of the group session when members tell others about their feelings, she shared fragmented memories of broken arms and legs and numerous hospital visits. She said
she remembered her father taking her to the hospital and telling
doctors that she was 'a tomboy, who was always climbing and
falling'. She told the group that she now remembered her father
frequently hitting her with a stick and breaking her limbs. Later
the therapist helped her to contact her older sister who confirmed
that their father had hit Isabel frequently and this was the reason
for her many hospital visits.*

THEORIES OF CHILD ABUSE

There are many theories which try to explain child abuse and we shall address a few in this chapter. One common theory, which is based largely on the work of Freud, and more recently on one of his followers, Erikson, considers that any form of ill-treatment, especially in the early stages of development, will affect a child and may cause behavioural difficulties and, possibly, developmental delay. This may be resolved if the child receives support and understanding from others. Some children, however, do not receive this support and, if the abuse is severe and constant, they may even repress the memories of it, as Isabel did. Such children, and those who remember but do not receive help, will have difficulties in future relationships, including those with their own children.

This theory has been, to a large extent, followed by many childcare organisations. During the early 1970s, when Ruth and Henry Kempe were discovering child abuse and formulating their 'Battered Baby Syndrome' in America, there was a wave of support and recognition from organisations such as the National Society for the Prevention of Cruelty to Children (NSPCC). It had existed in Britain since 1884 and had worked largely to prevent abuse by supporting overstressed parents and, occasionally, by removing children who were at risk. The work of the Kempes encouraged the NSPCC to start the National Advisory Centre on the Battered Child in London and to open Special units (first in Manchester and then around the country), led by a psychiatric social worker, John Pickett. These units helped parents, often very young people, to come to terms with their own childhood abuse and thus to resolve their difficulties with their own children.

Another theory of child abuse, which came to prominence during the late 1970s and early 1980s, was that of family dysfunction. Family therapists looked at the systems within a family and saw where there was an imbalance. The therapists usually saw the whole family together (often two or more therapists would be involved) and all would work to achieve 'homeostasis' or balance. This approach was also taken up by the NSPCC and where physical abuse occurred within a family workers would see all family members in order to make the family safe for the child or family.

This approach was popular, and worked well. It avoided the labelling or scapegoating of an abused child as the 'bad' or 'crazy' child. However, it ran into difficulties when sexual abuse was revealed to be a severe problem in many families, both in those where there was physical abuse and neglect and those where there was none. The family dysfunction approach ignored the abuse of power which is the main component of sexual abuse and in the early 1980s the feminist theory of child abuse gained prominence.

The feminist analysis was originally based on the premise that child sexual abuse is an abuse of power, and since almost all the known sexual abusers at that time were male, and the majority of abused children were female, this fitted with the view that a patriarchal society nurtured the abuse of male power over females. This view is still the baseline for feminist thinking on the subject and current debates on the proliferation of worldwide paedophile rings and child prostitution confirm that society in general easily ignores the sexual abuse of children. The feminist perspective also looks at the physical abuse of children, which is often perpetrated by females as well as males, and in which boys are more likely to be abused, and points to the high expectations upon women as mothers, to provide constant nurture for their offspring.

The child centred approach, which is the one I use, draws on the feminist analysis of the abuse of power as its baseline, but it looks at the imbalance of power between children and adults, rather than primarily between men and women. It accepts that the notion of women and children as property has fostered the power imbalance and it seeks to change that. Whilst equalising the balance of power between men and women may be seen as logical (now that geneticists have thrown doubt upon the superiority of the male), there are more difficulties where adults and children are concerned. While there is no doubt that children's intelligence is comparable with that of adults, no one can deny that their experience is less. A child within a society, and a family, has therefore to have boundaries and guidelines and has to receive education. This gives scope for adults to abuse their power against children. The child centred approach also draws heavily on the work of Alice Miller, especially *For Your Own Good – the roots of violence in child rearing* (1987a). She is a psychoanalyst who has now written many books pointing out the power abuse, 'poisonous pedagogy' and violence inherent in many child-rearing practices throughout the world. She traces the roots not only of her patients but of well-known power abusers such as Adolf Hitler and Josef Stalin to show that their violent child-hoods had an effect on their subsequent lives and upon whole nations.

MAKING SENSE OF THE THEORIES

Those who work constantly with children who have been abused need to have an awareness of the major theories of the causes of child abuse before they can look at the effects. Most of the theories suggest ways in which abuse may be perpetuated, either in families or within cultures. Childcare workers dealing with the survivors of abuse may have to help their young clients to ensure that they will have better non-abusive relationships with their own children. Of course, researchers are now discovering that physical and sexual abuse is much more widespread than was ever envisaged. It also seems, from research, that only about half of known sexual abusers have been sexually abused themselves, although the majority have been physically abused. It is also clear from research into workers in the helping professions, that many abused people spend their lives trying to alleviate the effects of abuse in others. However, those of us who are engaged in this work need to be clear that the work we do is focused upon the children rather than upon ourselves.

MODELS FOR UNDERSTANDING THE EFFECTS OF ABUSE

In my work I use one of two models to understand how abuse has affected the child and to guide my work with each particular child. The first model is based on a study of Post Traumatic Stress and so is most applicable to those children who are suffering in this way. It is also a model in which some understanding of the psychological processes of child development is necessary. The second model is very specific to child sexual abuse, as opposed to physical abuse, and it is a sociological model which is more appealing to those whose training is in this area.

Model 1 – information processing of trauma

Some abused children may suffer from Post Traumatic Stress for many years after the abusive events. Post Traumatic Stress Disorder is defined by the American Psychiatric Association. Their *Diagnostic and Statistical Manual of Mental Disorders (DSM–IV* 1994) lists the diagnostic criteria for PTSD, which I have simplified as follows:

- The person has been exposed to a traumatic event (or events) to which their response was fear, helplessness or horror (in children expressed as disorganised or agitated behaviour).

- The traumatic event(s) are re-experienced as
  (i) intrusive recollections of the events or, in children, by repetitive play, or
  (ii) distressing dreams, or, in children, frightening dreams without recognisable content, or
  (iii) 'flashbacks', or in children, re-enactment by them of the events in play, or
  (iv) intense psychological distress or physiological reactivity when exposed to cues which symbolise the events.

- There is persistent avoidance of stimuli associated with the trauma accompanied by numbing of responsiveness, and possibly by avoidance of thoughts and feelings about the trauma or of places connected with the trauma. Also inability to recall important aspects of the trauma and feelings of diminished interest in activities or detachment from others, inability to have loving feelings and no sense of future.

- There are persistent symptoms of increased arousal shown by sleep problems, outbursts of anger, concentration problems, hypervigilance and exaggerated startle response.

- Duration of disturbance is more than one month and it causes significant distress or impairment.

It is helpful that the APA has included the specific behaviours which children show, as opposed to adults, and this information has only been added to the definition of PTSD in recent years.

Post Traumatic Stress was first defined in the early 1980s, mainly by studying men exposed to battle conditions. The symptoms had, however, been noted in the First World War and called 'shell shock' and in the Second World War they were called 'battle fatigue'. Children who are suffering constant abuse, of whatever nature, are certainly 'on the front line', exposed to horrors as great as those on a battlefield. Their powerlessness, fear and horror have great parallels with other survivors – of torture, street or school shooting incidents, being taken hostage and so on. They cope in whatever ways they can. Sometimes these ways become dysfunctional and cause even greater problems for the child. Often children automatically change to different ways of coping, perhaps as they see these modelled by others. Sometimes they remain stuck in a cycle of coping which is ultimately self-destructive. The main function of therapy for such children is to offer alternative coping mechanisms and to help the child to reject existing mechanisms when she is able to do so.

In the last chapter we looked at coping mechanisms in order to assess how a child is currently functioning. My suggestion that an abused child's coping behaviour lies on a spectrum from victim to abuser is based on my own observations and also on the work of Carol Hartman and Ann Wolbert Burgess (1988). They looked at the data already available on Post Traumatic Stress and formulated their ideas on how the information from stressful events or trauma is processed by abused children. I have used this to devise Table 3.1 showing the consequences of trauma.

Phase 1 – pre-trauma

As we can see from Table 3.1, the process of the trauma is affected by the situation of the child pre-trauma. This is Phase 1 of the process. Experience now shows that very young children (below the age of two) who are constantly abused, are likely to suffer serious difficulties in development. At one time it was thought that because such young children seldom consciously re-membered their abuse, it would have no lasting effects. Workers with adolescents and adults, especially those who have been sexually abused, now know that difficulties are common. Simi-larly, older children, who have already suffered developmental delay, for whatever reason, are likely to be severely affected by later abuse.

John was eleven years old at referral. His self-esteem was ex-tremely low and he was not progressing well at school. He had been sexually abused by a convicted paedophile at the age of eight. John had lived in a loving foster home since he was ten years old. His mother had totally neglected him and sometimes physically abused him for as long as he could remember. He was the eldest child and had been born when his mother was only sixteen. He had subsequently had two half-sisters whom his mother treated well and whom he helped to care for. In an assessment session he painted a very angry picture, full of red and purple blotches. 'Why didn't my mother want me?' he asked the therapist, 'What's wrong with me?' The therapist was aware

Table 3.1 Consequences of trauma

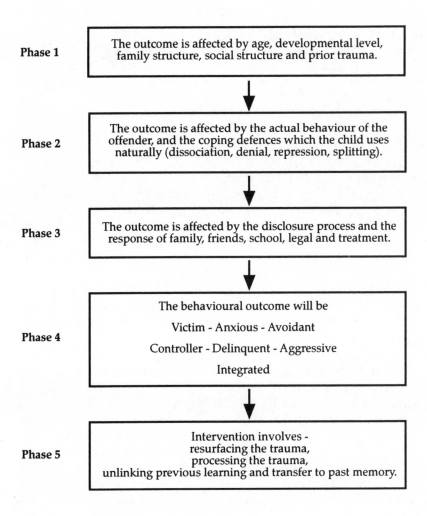

Phase 1 — The outcome is affected by age, developmental level, family structure, social structure and prior trauma.

Phase 2 — The outcome is affected by the actual behaviour of the offender, and the coping defences which the child uses naturally (dissociation, denial, repression, splitting).

Phase 3 — The outcome is affected by the disclosure process and the response of family, friends, school, legal and treatment.

Phase 4 — The behavioural outcome will be

Victim - Anxious - Avoidant

Controller - Delinquent - Aggressive

Integrated

Phase 5 — Intervention involves -
resurfacing the trauma,
processing the trauma,
unlinking previous learning and transfer to past memory.

that this early abusive treatment had made John more vulnerable to the paedophile, who had offered to play computer games with him. The sexual abuse he had suffered at that time went on for a year. His self-esteem was already so low that he felt he did not deserve the loving care of his foster mother but that he had deserved the abuse.

Phase 2 – the abusive act

In Phase 2 of Table 3.1, we see how the relationship with the offender, the style and type of abuse, and the frequency, all have an effect on the child. In addition, the amount of control which the child had will be important. For instance, a child who is being abused within the home will have very little control over this, especially if she is very young. This will probably lead to extreme feelings of helplessness and vulnerability and a lack of power in future relationships. Older children who are abused outside the home, like John in the above example, may have strong feelings of guilt because they feel they ought to have stopped the abuse. They wonder why they kept returning to the abuser and, of course, the abuser feeds into this by reminding the child that he has come of his own accord. The abuser will also tell the child that he is enjoying the abuse (even if there is pain) and because the child enjoys the attention, and sometimes the physical touching in the abusive behaviour, he feels even more guilty.

So the abuser, and the abuse, both affect the outcome, but in addition the way the child copes will also have an effect. For this reason, as we saw in the chapter on assessment, the child's coping mechanisms are important to understand.

Many people are familiar with the experience of dissociation from the body. For example, we often hear expressions such as, 'I was beside myself with anxiety', or 'It was almost as if it was happening to someone else and I was watching.' Terrible physical pain and torture can be withstood by those who are able to concentrate their whole being on something other than the pain. This is seen as a great virtue and skill and indeed it is. It is also something which most children are able to do instinctively. Fortunately most children do not have to suffer intense and continuous pain so this skill fades away as it is not used. Physically and sexually abused children may use dissociation frequently.

Kate was eleven and had been coming to therapeutic sessions for a few weeks. The therapist knew that she had been sexually and physically abused by both parents from an early age, and that they had served a prison sentence. She was in foster care but was not doing well at school. Teachers described a lack of concentration and Kate had been waiting for some time for a full educational assessment. In the fourth session Kate played with the doll's house, which she enjoyed. This time she arranged the furniture in a differ-

ent way from her earlier sessions and she picked up a small doll and placed it in one of the beds. 'What happens now?' asked the therapist. Kate made no reply. She picked up two larger dolls, a male and a female and placed them in the bedroom with the small doll. 'So now they are all in the bedroom', remarked the therapist, adopting a commentary rather than questioning. Kate still made no reply and for a minute or so she and the therapist sat in silence. Then Kate looked towards the therapist. 'Where were you just now?' the therapist asked. 'In the flowers', Kate replied, breaking up the bedroom scene and turning to some puppets. The therapist wondered silently if Kate was referring to flowers on wallpaper or curtains since adult survivors have often stated that they dissociated during abuse by concentrating on patterns in the room. She decided it was not helpful to question Kate at this time.

In fact by taking a careful history from the present carers and teachers the therapist saw that Kate had been dissociating for some time. Kate sometimes referred to 'Sarah', a girl of the same age who lived in her foster home. When Kate also referred to herself as Sarah and 'became' her in sessions the therapist discussed the matter with the foster mother and it was soon ascertained that Sarah did not exist. Kate's foster mother also described hearing Kate speaking in a loud, harsh voice, quite unlike her own and addressing passing neighbours or strangers in an abusive way. It seemed that Kate was showing the first signs of multiple personality disorder which is an extreme form of dissociation.

McElroy, writing in *Child Abuse & Neglect* (1992) suggests that dissociative disorders are perhaps the most complex and challenging disturbances commonly identified in survivors of child sexual abuse. She states that although adults may be diagnosed as having multiple personality disorder, children are often identified as having 'incipient multiple personality'. She gives reasons why it may be under-diagnosed and she gives two case examples of sexually abused children who are dissociating. Both of these examples give behaviour which is not unlike Kate's. The characters which she 'became' served useful purposes, either as controller (the loud voiced, aggressive personality) or as victim (Sarah).

By using the doll's house, and dolls, Kate had spontaneously used the psychodramatic method. She had recreated the place and circumstances of her abusive experiences and had used the mirror technique to see how she had coped with it. The therapist, therefore, continued to work with Kate in psychodramatic mode, addressing her 'personalities' or 'alters' directly. It appeared that

'Sarah' was the victim child, the one who was always to blame, the one who should be punished. The loud abusive person, named 'Jack' by Kate, was the controller. The therapist accepted these personalities and eventually 'Sarah' disappeared from the sessions. Kate used her foster mother much more as a supporter, as well as her therapist and eventually the foster mother reported that 'Jack' had disappeared too.

Lauren LaPorta, also writing in *Child Abuse & Neglect* (1992), gives a detailed case study of a nine-year-old girl whom she felt was suffering from incipient multiple personality disorder and whom she treated successfully within a period of about four months.

Kate's coping behaviours may be extreme but perhaps they are no more bizarre than total denial, or repression. This happens often with abused children and it may be difficult for adults to understand. The concept of repression was suggested by Freud but with regard to children the concept is fully explored by Erikson in *Childhood and Society* (1977). As we saw with Fiona, in chapter 2, a child can dissociate and also repress much of the abuse. Fiona had 'forgotten' the detail of her abuse, and may even have repressed the whole of it if she had not recorded it with the NSPCC at the time of disclosure. Her foster parents too had reminded her of the fact of her abuse, from time to time. In the past repression was sometimes seen as a 'healer' and children were encouraged to forget their experiences, which were never referred to. In the short term this may be valuable. Repression is a natural way of helping people to cope with the impossible. However, the feelings engendered by the abuse are not repressed and unless the trauma is processed the child will have strong feelings – of anger, sadness or guilt, for instance, which are inexplicable. Fiona was able to recover her memories, through psychodrama, and to make sense of her feelings.

Social workers who have been involved in investigations into paedophile rings will be familiar with boys who deny that they have been abused, even though their names have been given by several other children. Some of this denial, of course, may be due to shame because the child feels guilty. The abuser has encouraged the child to feel that he has deserved the abuse. Many adult males who have attended residential schools are now revealing their abuse by masters; abuse which they had repressed or denied because it had been given in the form of punishment for 'poor work' or 'bad behaviour' and they had felt that it was deserved. Some of these men, however, had not recognised it as abuse because it had been done in an atmosphere of 'cuddling' and 'pleasurable intimacy'. For young boys, away from their mothers for the first time, such intimate touching, when combined with caresses, would feel confusing, but the abuser would stress that the child had 'asked for it'.

This kind of denial or repression is understandable. Those who blank out the experience totally and recover the memories in adulthood face an atmosphere of disbelief, unless families will corroborate their stories.

Lorna was a young married woman who had been brought up strictly by very religious parents. At worship one day, with her husband and small children, she had an intense experience of anger towards the leader of their group, and she actually attacked him. In a therapeutic session the next day (Lorna had no previous history of psychiatric illness) she said that she had 'flipped back' to an experience when she was seven years old. She had been totally humiliated by her parents, and especially by her grandparents. She had told her mother, quite innocently, that her grandfather had been molesting her. The grandfather, who was a religious leader, had denied it and his whole religious group had combined to denounce Lorna as a liar.

Inadvertently, in the informal worship of the previous day, the scene had been recreated physically and also, to some extent, emotionally, as Lorna had felt humiliated by something the leader had said. Just as in psychodrama the scene can be recreated deliberately, it was, in this case, recreated accidentally. Lorna had repressed the whole incident, and with it, her sexual abuse. At the therapist's suggestion, and with her husband's support, she spoke to her uncle, her mother's brother. He reminded her of an incident when the grandfather had molested Lorna's cousin during a family party and had been caught in the act by the child's father, Lorna's uncle. The grandparents had moved away and there had been no further contact. Lorna was an adolescent by then but this incident had not reminded her of her own abuse and neither had any family member spoken to her about it, or apologised for their previous behaviour. The uncle and other family members then corroborated Lorna's early memory.

By continuing to work psychodramatically with the therapist for a few sessions Lorna was able to come to terms with her experiences and she said that she had a better relationship with her own children as a result.

Another coping mechanism is splitting, which we have already discussed in chapter 2. A healthy baby uses splitting to protect the good from the bad until she has learned to integrate the two, in herself and others. An abused child finds it impossible to integrate and divides the world into good and bad.

Mark's teachers and foster parents were at the end of their tethers. His classroom behaviour was disruptive. He was rude, aggressive and inattentive. He had no friends and it was clear that he was unhappy himself and was making all those around him unhappy. His school behaviour was particularly frustrating as he had been assessed by an educational psychologist as well above average. He was ten years old and until he was seven he had been physically abused and neglected by his parents. He was brought to the attention of the authorities (at seven) because he deliberately ran in front of a bus and told nurses that he wanted to kill himself. In the therapy session he was restless and anxious. He wrote some words on a sheet of paper and cut them out. 'STUPID' was the first word. He took a piece of sticky tape and stuck the word to his forehead. He looked at himself in the mirror and glanced over towards the therapist. 'That's right, isn't it?' he challenged. 'I don't know', she replied. 'It's not a word I use.'

It took Mark many months before he began to accept that he had any good characteristics or to accept that others (the therapist, his foster mother) were not perfect. He also dissociated severely. He was already committing delinquent acts which had brought him to the attention of the police. Mark was not simply living up to the expectations of his parents, or accepting the labelling of teachers or his peer group. He had split off the 'good' parts of himself and projected them onto others, and he had introjected the 'bad' parts of others. Mark's foster mother (who was a single woman with no other foster children) was prepared to work with Mark, and the therapist, to help him to recreate his earliest years and to reintegrate his personality. It was an uphill struggle which may have seemed unrewarding to an observer. Mark's foster mother was, however, a 'good-enough' mother and he had formed a good attachment. Probably Mark will never achieve his full potential but there have been no more suicide attempts.

Phase 3 – disclosure and responses

It is possible that some children never reveal their abuse to anyone and that only the child and the abuser know about it. This may be very rare, however, even in sexual abuse, which is the most secret type. In neglect, and in emotional and physical abuse there are usually other family members or members of the community who are aware of what is happening but who feel powerless or afraid to act. Young children sometimes innocently reveal all kinds of abuse, including sexual, especially if the abuser is confident that the child will not be believed (as we saw with Lorna). Adults find it difficult or impossible to believe when children do talk about abusive behaviour. If a child complains to her mother that her father is 'messing about' it is unusual for that mother to suspect abuse. Contrary to popular opinion, that attitude is also the norm amongst social workers, teachers and health workers. As Robert Dingwall points out (in Stainton Rogers, Hevey and Ash 1989) the 'rule of optimism' prevails not only in child protection issues. It is a natural response to an organisational and psychological problem. Occasionally this rule is overcome and child protection workers try to screen all potentially abusive behaviour. They are then labelled 'over-zealous' or even 'vindictive', as was demonstrated in 1987 in Cleveland, UK, when medical and social workers were reviled for taking a pessimistic view of symptoms of possible sexual abuse which children were displaying.

Most children, in my experience, have tried to talk to someone about their abuse. Usually they have been ignored or told that they must have misunderstood or been mistaken. Since children are often told this, most of them accept the abusive behaviour as justified. If the abuser has been challenged, further threats or bribes may be given to the child. Sometimes abusers challenge the child themselves. In physical abuse the abuser may ask the child whether he deserves the 'punishment'. The child usually agrees and the abuser has justified his own distorted cognition and passed this on to the child. In adulthood, the victim repeats this distortion as he says, 'I got plenty of beatings and it never did me any harm.' This is often said by those who are now abusing others or who have had difficulties in relationships. The same distorted cognition can happen in sexual abuse. The abuser may ask the child, 'Do you think there is anything wrong with this?' The child, who cannot make an informed judgement or give informed consent, denies her innermost feelings. This denial of feelings often lasts a lifetime. She feels she has 'got it wrong', that she is unable to name her feelings. Like Belinda, whom we met in chapter 2, she does not know what she is feeling or even who she is.

As those who work with abusive adults know, this cognitive distortion is difficult to change. It is also difficult to change it in the victims of abuse. The child's perception of self and others is distorted, not only by the abuser, but sometimes by family and friends, by school and the authorities and, not least, by the legal system and the courts. Fortunately there are many examples of children who have been supported by family, friends and child protection workers so that they can be witnesses for the prosecution against their abusers. Such support may be misconstrued as 'coaching' by the Crown Prosecution Service and professionals must be extremely careful that their therapeutic support does not involve any reconstruction of events which are the subject of criminal proceedings. Indeed the CPS has power to prevent such support if they feel it would be prejudicial.

A child who has been systematically abused, however, will have accepted many of the abuser's own cognitive distortions, and in addition will almost certainly feel powerless, afraid and vulnerable. An adversarial legal system must allow the abuser, or his representative, to cross-examine the witness. Despite all the safeguards which have been introduced to help the child (video presentation of the evidence-in-chief, the use of screens or video in cross-examination and so on), the scales are weighted heavily against an abused child. To protect the civil rights of those who are accused this may be a fair system. For a child or adult whose sense of self has already been destroyed by the abuser, the system is far from adequate.

In working with abused children, therefore, we need to take all these outside influences into consideration and to understand how they have affected the child. Unravelling all the components in this process can be a complicated and time-consuming business.

Phase 4 – behavioural outcome

By the time the child is referred for therapy the behavioural outcome or the consequences of the trauma are well apparent.

As we saw in chapter 2, abused children's behaviour tends to lie on a spectrum between controller and victim, unless the child has already managed to integrate the abusive experience. Most children will try out different behaviours and many will identify with the same-sex parent (as do many unabused children). Thus a female child with a passive or victimised mother is likely to behave in victimised ways which make her more vulnerable, not only to her abuser, but to bullies and other abusers. In addition, a female child may be fed with stereotypes of female behaviour so that assertive behaviour becomes even more difficult.

A typical example of accepting the victim position was shown by Nancy, aged twelve. She wore her coat, with the hood up, throughout the session. Her hair obscured most of the rest of her face. She was tall and well-built and her adolescent development had added to her size. She was obviously embarrassed about this. She was reluctant to leave her social worker who had brought her to the sessions. The therapist knew that Nancy had been abused by her mother's brother, who had lived with Nancy's mother in an incestuous relationship. Nancy's siblings had also been abused. She accepted all the worker's suggestions and played with the doll's house in the manner of a younger child. Eventually she set up a scene with the dolls where a male doll 'touched' a girl doll who told her mother about it. The mother said, 'Never mind, I'll tell him off tomorrow.' Nancy looked helplessly at the therapist. Her despair and resignation were almost unbearable.

The work which had to be done with Nancy was, of course, to encourage her to try out more assertive behaviour and to try and change her understanding that being abused was inevitable. Her own mother had modelled a similar position for Nancy and she found it difficult to change. One of her younger brothers, aged four, took a much more aggressive stance and hurled himself at the therapist, headbutting her in a painful manner as he entered the room. Most therapists are prepared for some children to be aggressive but when Olivia, aged fifteen, came to sessions, the therapist was taken aback by her threatening behaviour.

Olivia's father was in a managerial position in a prominent public service. He had sexually abused her for about half her life and had eluded punishment although his wife had divorced him long ago. Olivia wore all black clothes and all white make-up. She had apparently requested therapy herself but it was soon clear that the therapist was not going to have an easy time. She volunteered the information that she 'sometimes did drugs or booze'. She looked defiantly at the therapist as she said this. She took out a metal nail file and casually filed a long red finger nail. Then she pointed the file at the therapist who was asking her about schoolfriends. 'Everyone knows', she said slowly, moving the nail file for emphasis, 'there's no messing with Olivia'.

Olivia's controlling behaviour was impressive but was preventing her from showing vulnerability and therefore preventing her from accepting help from her mother or her therapist. Eventually a

supportive friend helped her to drop some of her bravado and she
became accessible for therapeutic work.

Phase 5 – intervention

The last phase of this model involves 'resurfacing' the trauma.
Psychodrama and dramatherapy are particularly useful in helping a
child or adult re-enact details of the abuse, in a safe way, over
which they have control. This, in itself, is therapeutic since the
subconscious memories more usually intrude in the form of
dreams and nightmares where the dreamer has no control. Once
the child sees that the memories can be controlled by herself and
when she sees also that the therapist understands what has happened, then she can start to process the traumatic events.

The therapist can use the model to throw light on the child's
behaviour, to explain distorted cognition, and to reassure. Again,
action methods may be used very effectively to illustrate the
explanations. For a child who is full of fear a dramatherapeutic
approach (using metaphor) is helpful, especially in the first instance. The child re-learns the traumatic experience and so the
behavioural outcome is different. Even quite young children understand that this 'sorting out' is necessary and important. When this
is done the trauma can be transferred to past memory, where it
will not be intrusive, and the child can learn to live again.

Model 2 – traumagenic dynamics

A model which is more specific to child sexual abuse was formulated by Finkelhor and Browne (1985). It suggests that there are
four dynamics within the experience of being sexually abused as a
child that cause distorted learning and thinking and which, therefore, lead directly to difficult behaviour as the child copes with the
distortions. The four dynamics are:

1. Traumatic sexualisation   3. Betrayal

2. Stigmatisation   4. Powerlessness

In my experience most sexually abused children who are referred
for behavioural difficulties will show some problems in at least
three of the areas.

1. Traumatic sexualisation

During sexual abuse the child's learning about sexuality is distorted as she may be encouraged to exchange sexual activity for care and attention, to perform sexual acts inappropriate to development and she may associate sex with negative emotions, pain or punishment. This can lead to confusion about sexual identity and sexual norms and sometimes an aversion to, or an excessive preoccupation with, sexual activity. In extreme cases there may be sexual aggression, prostitution and sexual dysfunction or phobias.

In chapter 6 we will look at children who are sexually aggressive since work with these children is specialised and somewhat different from working with children who are more obviously victims. Children who are used as prostitutes will also be inappropriately sexualised. Members of the public, and even some professionals, may find it difficult to understand why an eleven-year-old boy or girl should ask for money for 'sex' and should do this so casually. A child who has become sexualised by their own early abuse may turn to prostitution as a form of false control, believing that they are likely to be abused by adults anyway and that to take money is the only form of control. In addition, of course, many sexually abused children are initially abused within the home. They then run away and, their vulnerability increased by their earlier abuse and by their homeless state, they are picked up by pimps or adult prostitutes. Therapy with such children is difficult. There may be frequent 'lapses' and sometimes therapy is not resumed until adulthood, when the urge to make closer relationships is more pressing.

Sexual dysfunction and phobias usually become more problematic as children become adults, but if a child appears to present with traumatic sexualisation there is often a great deal of guilt and shame which is compounded by a lack of knowledge about sexuality. Sexual education can be the way forward to assist children to look at the reasons for their particular difficulties.

2. Stigmatisation

It is common for sexual abusers to denigrate and blame the child for the abuse. They rationalise their own behaviour with comments like, 'It's because you are so pretty', and so on. The abuser also insists on secrecy and this adds to the shame. As we have seen in the previous model, the reactions of others upon disclosure can also add to shameful feelings and a stereotypical label of 'damaged goods'. The guilt, shame and low self-esteem which this produces may lead to isolation, drug or alcohol abuse, self-mutilation or even suicide. Therapists should not ignore suicide attempts, or assume that they are accidents, even in children as young as six. Building self-esteem is an essential part of rehabilitation for a child who is feeling stigmatised.

Recognising low self-esteem in a young person is not always easy. When we were introduced to Olivia, the fifteen-year-old, whose example we quoted to show extreme control, we may not have recognised that she was suffering from stigma and low self-esteem. An intelligent girl, from a middle-class family, she felt different from most of her friends. She attempted to rationalise that difference by her choice of friends and her interest in the drug culture. In fact she felt the stigma of being a sexually abused child keenly and the therapeutic work she did subsequently emphasised her self-worth.

3. Betrayal

This is a very powerful dynamic which is produced as trust is abused and vulnerability is exploited, often by those whom the child expected to give care and protection. This produces a great sadness, often extreme grieving and depression. Anger, mistrust and hostility often follow the grief. Such children may become clingy, vulnerable to further abuse, isolated or aggressive and may have great difficulty in forming relationships. Children who feel betrayed may become adults whose need for security is so great that any break-up of a relationship is seen as a betrayal. Simply listening to and witnessing the child's pain will be helpful. Building up their self-worth so that they do not feel that they deserve to be betrayed will also help. Depression in children can also be ignored by professionals or treated with medication alone. Although medication may be helpful in the short term, children who feel betrayed need to express their grief and anger because otherwise the depression will recur.

4. Powerlessness

This dynamic exists in all kinds of abuse but in sexual abuse is particularly potent because the body is invaded against the child's wishes. Force, trickery or bribery may be used, so the child is constantly and overwhelmingly fearful. The powerlessness is increased if no one believes that the abuse happened. This leads to the behaviour discussed earlier, where the child may identify with the aggressor and become very controlling or perceive herself as a victim and become even more vulnerable. Fear is the most obvious outcome of this dynamic and this may produce dissociation, running away, truancy, bullying and delinquency. Powerlessness is a feeling which exists in all abused children and can be addressed firstly by acknowledging it as a fact, by addressing the fear which is the natural outcome of powerlessness and, eventually, by assertiveness training.

Finkelhor and Browne's model is especially useful in practical situations where a child shows a clear behavioural outcome of the abuse. Looking, with the child, at the fearful or shameful feelings can make them more manageable and help to dispel their continuing power. Many years after the abuse has finished these feelings persist and it is as if the abuser still has power over the abused child. Supporting the child to overcome this herself is a major part of therapy. In the following chapters some suggestions and examples of how this might be accomplished will be given.

4   CREATING SAFETY AND MAKING BOUNDARIES: THE USE OF TOYS AND EQUIPMENT

> It should be noted that children at play are not playing about:
> their games should be seen as their most serious-minded activity.
>
> Montaigne

Many abused children have low expectations of adults. They expect that the adults will further abuse them in one way or another. The only uncertainty is when it will be. Adults who are not familiar with working in this area sometimes assume that abusive adults are somehow 'different' from others, and certainly from them. They either assume that the child will perceive this instantly (perhaps because they believe that their role, as doctor, teacher, etc. gives immunity) or they try immediately to show the child that they are different from their own adult perception of an abusive person. Unfortunately their over-friendliness, permissiveness and indulgence often mirror precisely the initial behaviour of abusive adults the child has known.

In a recent piece of research where children were asked about their social workers (Bannister & Gallagher 1995) one boy said approvingly, 'They asked me what I wanted and they really listened.' A girl said, despairingly, 'I didn't want them to do anything, just to listen.' Listening, of course, may be harder than it seems. Children are usually more perceptive than adults about the nuances of expression, in face, body and voice, and they soon sense whether an adult is really interested in them, and therefore really listening, or whether the adult is only interested in certain aspects of what they may say. Young people may not be experienced enough to make accurate judgements about relationships but they usually respond to a calm, warm approach which is not overwhelming or overbearing.

KNOWING YOURSELF AND THE CHILD

Understanding one's own motives for working with abused children is a vital part of knowing yourself. Knowing yourself makes it far easier to be honest and straightforward with children. Natural warmth, a sense of discovery, creative spontaneity and a firm belief in the capabilities and strengths of children are important foundations for this work. In the childcare professions personal motivation and understanding are addressed to a greater or lesser degree during training. All qualified psychotherapists will have had some personal therapy as an integral part of their training. For others this self-knowledge may have grown with maturity or in personal study. Many of us will have looked at our own coping mechanisms as we learn about controlling or victimised behaviour in those who have been abused. Alice Miller believes that most of us have been abused in one way or another. In *For Your Own Good* (1987a) she uses the expression 'poisonous pedagogy' to describe the controlling behaviour which many parents use in the guise of teaching the child. She points out that many restraints are unnecessary and that they stifle creativity and self-reliance. Restraints may come disguised as 'care' but they may be an effort to prove superiority or just a covert way of abusing power.

It is true that many adults who physically, sexually and emotionally abuse children rationalise this by making statements about teaching good behaviour or widening children's education. The title *For Your Own Good* which Miller uses, expresses clearly the sentiments made by bullies who severely punish children for their own gratification. Many abusive adults have so rationalised their own abusive behaviour that they have convinced themselves that they really are 'doing it for the child's own good'. To work therapeutically with such adults, to help them to understand their own motivation, is a long uphill struggle.

On the other hand, a lack of restraint and a failure to observe and enforce a child's boundaries of behaviour are equally damaging in the formation of a therapeutic relationship. Children deserve their privacy just as adults do. They are also entitled to make mistakes within a safe environment, without being punished. Perhaps the idea of 'containment' gives a clearer understanding of the therapeutic relationship. If a child tries to project out the painful, difficult areas of his life his behaviour will become problematic, unless someone can help him to contain this in a therapeutic way. For a child to know that the therapist can accept all the revolting nastiness of the trauma, without rejecting the child, and that the therapist can contain this without damaging herself, is to create a healing situation.

Peter was five years old and had already had two sessions with his therapist. He had explored the puppets, the drawing materials and the collection of small animals. Peter had greeted his therapist on their first session by 'headbutting' her rather painfully in the abdomen. She had told him quietly but firmly that hurting people was not allowed in the sessions. He was not to hurt her and she would not hurt him either. He had kicked menacingly at a large floorcushion as she told him this but he had not repeated the headbutting behaviour. In the second session, whilst playing with a crocodile puppet, Peter had picked up a small plastic sword and declared his intention of killing the rabbit puppet which he had placed on the therapist's hand. Swiftly she had dropped the puppet onto a floor cushion and allowed Peter to hit the rabbit in a way which did not harm her. He stopped after two strokes of his sword. Peter's main interest had been in the 'dressing-up box' and on this third session he wore a feathered head-dress and placed another similar one on the therapist's head. 'You make the dinner', he commanded. 'I'm going to mend the fences.' Carefully he built a fence with floor cushions around the perimeter of the room, enclosing himself and the therapist. He 'banged in' imaginary fence posts with the flat of his sword. The therapist stirred the pot with a 'stick' made from rolled-up newspaper, bound with tape. 'Peter's mending the fences', she commented, 'so the wild animals can't get in. That's good, we'll be safe. This dinner smells good.'

Peter's barricade was nearly complete but he had run out of floor cushions. He tried to drag the doll's house into the gap and in doing so the removable roof came away in his hands and he fell over. Instinctively the therapist stood up, from her cross-legged position on the floor, to check if he was hurt. 'Stir the dinner', screamed Peter, loudly and urgently, 'Stir the dinner!' Obediently she sat down, recognising that to step out of role would be to damage Peter's carefully mended fences and to break the boundaries.

Although he was only five years old Peter was already in a very controlling mode. He was the youngest child and the only boy in a family of four children. All four had been physically and sexually abused by both parents and by other adult members of the extended family. There were no boundaries, no fences and no safe places in Peter's life. For him, adult behaviour was inexplicable and unpredictable. Physical abuse could follow a nurturing act such as the provision of a meal. Sexual abuse was presented sometimes as a 'grown-up treat' for complicity, or as 'punishment' for failure to complete tasks. Peter had constructed his own rules in an effort to make some sense of the chaos. Making sense of the chaos is a task which all therapists with children recognise. 'Let's try to sort this out', is a reassuring phrase which gives children hope that it can, indeed, be sorted. Their fear is that it is impossible to make sense of the situation and therefore one must control it rigidly or repress it and deny its existence.

A recent television programme looked at the disaster of Aberfan in South Wales, thirty years after the event. In Aberfan the spoil tip from the coalmine became unstable because of water and within minutes it descended upon the town of Aberfan, engulfing the school and claiming a whole generation of children's lives.

A young woman who had survived the disaster said that for four years she had held the events inside her, unable to give them a voice. Eventually, in adolescence, she undertook her own therapy by writing pages and pages which described the whole incident and her feelings about it. The chaos must be sorted out and this child, like many others, had healed herself, although she must have suffered indescribably for many years until she was able to do it. Unlike many abused children, she had the advantage of a loving family who supported and helped her, even though they must have been grieving for the whole town. It is this kind of unconditional support, which does not probe, and is prepared to wait, that an abused child needs.

MAKING AGREEMENTS

Giving a child like Peter a clear explanation of what is happening and what is going to happen, as far as possible, is one way of establishing clear boundaries. Answering a child's questions is not always enough since many children will be afraid to ask or they will assume that they will not be given the information. They may also make assumptions based on misinformation which is given to them by parents and carers. It is therefore important that there is always an initial planning meeting with parents/carers, the child and the therapist. The issues concerning treatment of siblings or groups of children will be discussed in the next chapter but in most cases it is better to see an individual child with parents and without other siblings at the planning stage. If a child has been referred through another professional it is sometimes possible for that person (usually the child's social worker) to be present at the planning meeting. Other professionals may be represented only by their letter of referral but therapists should request permission to discuss the referral letter with the parents and child if appropriate. This can open the discussion to the expectations of the referrer about the therapy and then the parents/carers can be encouraged to discuss their own expectations and perhaps their reservations too. Sometimes, depending on the age and personality of the child, this will provide an opportunity for joining the discussion to name worries and fears and for the therapist to give explanations and to state her own expectations. Agreements about practical matters such as frequency and number of sessions, payment if appropriate, and who accompanies the child to sessions can be made at this stage.

It helps to keep boundaries if a set number of sessions is agreed upon, followed by a review, with a further number of sessions if necessary. Agreements with parents and child at this stage must also include an understanding that whatever the child says to the therapist is confidential unless the child chooses otherwise. Of course, it must be made clear that the child is quite free to share with anyone so there is no cult of secrecy. It is usually helpful to raise the question of the support or therapy which the parents/carers are receiving and to remind them that the child's therapeutic sessions may be painful and that the child will need extra support and nurture while they are progressing.

AN AGREEMENT WITH A CHILD

Once a child feels comfortable with an adult, and after clear explanations have been given and opinions heard, it is time to make an agreement. Children and parents make contracts or agreements frequently; bed times, meal times are negotiated and agreed. Homework is done so there is time for play, or television viewing. A therapist will find that if a child is allowed to make a list of subjects to be discussed then the adult can add to this and mutual agreement can be reached. For younger children or those with learning difficulties, pictures can help.

Nine-year-old Quentin had some learning difficulties. He drew a baby, a male figure and a large building for his agreement. He explained that he agreed to talk about his baby sister, his stepfather and about school. His therapist drew a small male figure on the same piece of paper and said she also needed to talk about Matthew at some stage. Matthew was a boy at school whom Quentin had assaulted. Quentin appeared to have been bullying Matthew for some time and he looked challengingly at the therapist as she drew the small figure. The therapist repeated her point. 'At some stage we have to talk about this because it's causing you problems.' 'I didn't do anything', replied Quentin. 'Not now', replied the therapist, 'but we need to talk about it when you are ready'. 'OK', he agreed. 'Later, then.' The difficult subject was placed on the agenda making it easier to introduce later on when Quentin and the therapist had built some trust. To ignore it at this stage would have been dishonest since both Quentin and the therapist knew that it was this behaviour which had triggered Quentin's referral.

Older children sometimes need agreements about the kind of toys or equipment they will use or the areas of activity in which they will engage. Some children have been made anxious by other adults about certain activities such as drawing and painting or singing. They protest that they are 'no good' at such creative activities and they need to be reassured that they will not be forced to do them. This is the point when the therapist is grateful for an eclectic training and approach.

On learning that her worker was a dramatherapist, twelve-year-old Rosie looked stunned. 'No acting', she said firmly. 'I can't. It's stupid anyway, kids' stuff.' 'No problem', replied the therapist, 'how about you making up a story instead?' Storymaking is used extensively in dramatherapy and Rosie had no difficulty in telling a story about a girl called Annie who told her mother exactly what she thought of her. In telling the story Rosie effectively took the roles of mother and daughter in a way which helped her to look at the problem she was having in accepting that her mother had neglected and eventually abandoned her.

Differences in gender and culture may cause some children to be reluctant to take part in certain activities or use some kinds of equipment.

Sharnaz was a young Asian woman whose mother had died recently. After her death Sharnaz's father had sexually abused

Sharnaz and her younger sister. Although Sharnaz's English was perfect she found it difficult to speak directly to her therapist. She moved quickly to a chair and sat quietly, twisting a lock of her long hair around her beringed fingers. The therapist sat in comfortable silence for a while and then admired one of Sharnaz's rings. Sharnaz smiled shyly. The therapist asked her to take a look around the room to see if there was anything she was interested in. Sharnaz did not move from her seat but her eyes flickered uneasily over art materials, cushions, doll's house, and settled on a set of Asian rag dolls. There were eight dolls in this extended family set. The therapist pointed out that the females in the family were wearing 'shalwar kameez', and asked if Sharnaz ever wore this. She wore her school uniform for the sessions. Sharnaz nodded. The therapist picked up the 'mother' doll and brought it to Sharnaz to look at the attractive clothing. Sharnaz stroked the shining black braid of hair which hung down the doll's back. 'My mother had hair like this.'

Once Sharnaz had begun to trust she was able to make an agreement that she would talk about her mother although she had apparently been unable to do this before. In fact she became able to hold psychodramatic conversations with her dead mother and to commence her process of grieving. She was afraid of the spirit of her mother who she thought may punish her for 'allowing' her father to abuse her and her sister. The white therapist was able to work within the metaphor of the spirit in a way which was acceptable to Sharnaz.

USING TOYS AND EQUIPMENT

One way to lose the boundaries of a session is to fill the room with so many toys that some children rush around frantically trying to use them all. It is better to have a small selection of carefully chosen toys than to have too many distracting and irrelevant items of equipment. The first rule is to choose items with which the therapist feels comfortable and for which there is a clear creative use. Interactive equipment is also necessary so computer games to be played alone are not helpful. Board games for two people can sometimes be useful for certain children, specially designed board games in particular, but sometimes games can be used as distractions and diversions both by child and therapist. A few quick games of noughts and crosses or hangman are often sufficient to establish rapport with a child who loves games. Developmentally, six- and seven-year-olds like to prove their prowess with these games, just as four- and five-year-olds love to play card games like 'pairs'.

Most young children will appreciate dolls, dolls' cots and dolls' houses, though some boys will disdain these. Many pre-pubescent and adolescent girls will find these toys comforting and useful, however. In caring for a baby doll, dressing, 'feeding' or bathing it, a child may express her own needs and wishes for herself or perhaps her anxiety about younger siblings.

Tim was a seven-year-old boy who was fascinated by the dolls in the therapy room and soon settled down to play with them when he was sure that he had permission and that they were not 'only for girls'. He had been brought up in a loving but rather repressive household where sexual matters were not discussed and where gender roles were rigidly defined. He had been sexually abused, along with two other seven-year-olds, by a group of adolescent boys. It was another of the victims who disclosed abuse and Tim felt, quite correctly, that he could not talk about it to his mother because she would be shocked and hurt, nor to his father, who would be angry. Tim became more and more depressed and withdrawn and both teachers and his mother complained that they could not reach him. He had no means of knowing whether the female therapist would be shocked too but he picked up a boy doll and told the therapist that he was naughty 'because he took his clothes off'. The therapist wondered when it was 'OK to take your clothes off', and they discussed this. Tim added 'What if a big boy tells him to?' The therapist agreed that it would be difficult for the little boy to protest. Tim took over the role of big boy ordering the little boy about. He was unable to play this role well and he asked the therapist to help and to 'scare the little boy doll'. The therapist made loud noises and threatening gestures. Tim nodded and pointed to the little boy doll. 'He likes being scared.'

Tim was exploring his confusion about the pleasure and pain of his abuse. He was also asking the therapist to role model an aggressive personality which was alien to his own gentle personality but which he sometimes wished he could use for himself. Eventually he was able to act out the abuse more specifically and to explore it sufficiently to relegate it from its prominent position in his life. His mother was also helped to talk to Tim in a more open way about his feelings.

Dolls' houses, with furniture and miniature people can be used in many ways, some of them unexpected. Therapists should not assume that children are necessarily repeating actual events and they should be careful about interpreting scenes which children depict in doll's house play. Sturdy furniture is usually best as broken and damaged toys only confirm to abused children that they do not deserve good materials.

Viv had been brought up by her grandmother after her mother abandoned her when she was less than twelve months old. Grandmother had died after a short illness shortly after Viv's fourth birthday and she was now in foster care. She played constantly with the doll's house, putting a doll in a bed and saying that it was poorly, or sometimes, that it was dead.

The therapist allowed her to play this theme through several sessions, introducing variations, showing that some sick people recovered and others did not. After some time the foster mother reported that she seemed more settled and was able to talk about her grandmother more easily.

Puppets are probably more versatile than dolls. Animal puppets are popular with both boys and girls as are archetypal figures such as witches and kings and queens. A small bear or rabbit puppet can be the child's friend throughout the sessions and scenarios can be enacted with these or with fairytale figures which will create distance between the child's actual situation and his or her expression of it.

Puppets have been known for centuries and are fascinating to young and old alike. Children will sometimes use them in a very theatrical manner, setting up a 'puppet show' over the back of a chair or from behind a curtain. They can enact all the parts, speak all the voices and feel invisible as the therapist's eye and ear are drawn to the moving puppet. If these sessions are captured on video (and most children are happy to give consent and to help set up equipment) additional material can be gained from observing the child as he performs as 'lion' or as 'lamb'.

Most children can play a role convincingly as a puppet, although they may be quite unable to play that role in life. A direct psychodramatic representation of a desired role may be too threatening for children who cannot, therefore, act out the more assertive role they desire to play. The puppet which they manipulate can, however, play the role for them. If children are allowed to watch videotapes of their own puppet performances they can begin to accept that they are capable of being more assertive and they can then assimilate the role. As Moreno said, 'Roles do not emerge from the self, but the self may emerge from roles.'

Will was only nine but he had established a reputation for aggressive behaviour. The full extent of his abuse was not known but it included physical and sexual abuse by several people. He picked up a crocodile puppet, with large teeth, and began to menace the therapist with it, swooping it down past her face and barely missing it. The therapist modelled a vulnerable role, picking up a fluffy blue rabbit puppet and allowing it to show fear by shaking and muttering that it felt scared of the crocodile. Will looked scornfully at the rabbit and continued his terrifying behaviour, forcing the rabbit to jump out of the way. The play continued until the crocodile and the rabbit (and Will and the therapist) were exhausted and Will flopped down on a cushion, still holding the crocodile. The therapist picked up a dog puppet with her other hand and spoke to the rabbit. 'Let's tell the croc where to go', suggested the dog to the rabbit. The crocodile was surprised when the dog growled at him and even more surprised when the rabbit, safely behind the dog, told the crocodile to clear off, in a very firm voice. The crocodile responded with louder roars and more aggressive snapping then suddenly Will slipped the puppet off his hand and slid it under a floor cushion. 'It's under a stone', he said, 'I've squashed it. Can I have the rabbit for a bit?'

Will was a very frightened little boy who was too afraid to show his vulnerability because he knew that it was likely that he would be abused again if he did so. In the enactment with the puppets he saw that the therapist was not afraid to show her fear and that she coped with it by seeking a supporter, the assertive dog. He was also able to see the therapist playing more than one role and in subsequent sessions Will was able to reveal more of his vulnerable role and to develop his assertive and non-aggressive roles. He used the rabbit as a supporter throughout the sessions and was eventually given a tiny plastic rabbit, to keep in his pocket when he felt the need of support in real-life situations.

One of the most difficult issues in working with abused children is whether the therapist should touch a child, other than formally – in a handshake for instance – or in order to restrain in an emergency. It is true that non-sexual touching can sometimes feel threatening or be misinterpreted by a child. On the other hand some abused children, who have lived in children's homes where 'no touching' was the rule, have said that they felt that they were untouchable. However, many abused children cannot bear to be touched and the therapist should always ask herself, before touching a child for comfort, whether the comfort is really for the child's benefit or for the therapist's. (This issue is discussed further in chapter 7.)

Will, as we have seen, enjoyed using the puppets because they gave the necessary distance to the work he had to do. He could not bear anyone to touch him directly, although he had been inadvertently touched through puppets in much of the energetic play described above. During a puppet enactment of a dragon killing a crocodile (which he had acted alone, with a puppet on each hand) he became distressed and said 'there are too many crocodiles about'. He sank into a corner of the room and closed his eyes. The therapist remained silent for some minutes and then she picked up the rabbit and said 'Rabbit wants you to know that he is here.' Will remained silent but opened his eyes. The therapist moved closer to sit by his side and said 'Rabbit likes to be stroked when he is feeling bad.' Will smiled and reached out to stroke the puppet, which remained on the therapist's hand. 'Mm,' said Rabbit, 'good. Want me to stroke your arm?' Will nodded and smiled slightly while Rabbit stroked his arm. After this session his foster mother reported that he had asked for a cuddle, along with the other foster children, for the first time.

Drawing materials, paints and modelling clay are popular with most children. From finger painting to the modelling and painting of sophisticated figures, young people of all ages can participate in some level of creative activity. As we saw in earlier chapters, children like Beattie, who are severely developmentally delayed, can benefit from the unrestrained use of paints. Children like Alan, who have been sensorially deprived and who have never fully experienced embodiment play, can use Play Doh or clay to replay their missing experiences. Older children may use drawing to express what is happening to them.

Yasmin, aged six, began her series of drawings with a witch, a witch in a hole. She said the witch was frightened and lonely but she could not get out of the hole which was in the garden of a house. The therapist said she felt sorry that the witch was frightened and lonely. Yasmin drew the house and a green monster who came out of the house. The monster, she said, had lots of children but they all died. She drew bars over the monster and said it was in prison. When the monster was safely in prison Yasmin drew another picture of the witch who had now come out of the hole and who wandered in the garden where she met a ghost. She gave her cloak and hat to the ghost who flew away with them, on the witch's broomstick. Yasmin's final picture in this series, which was drawn over several weeks, was of a baby who lay in the garden, amongst the flowers, with a rainbow overhead. A red arc grew out of the garden and the therapist asked Yasmin about it. 'That's the bridge I have to go over', Yasmin answered.

Yasmin had been sexually abused by her father who had told her that she was 'evil' and 'possessed' and that she was a witch. Her mother had been unable to help her. It was a long time before Yasmin felt ready to 'go over the bridge' and to live outside the shadow of the house in which she had been abused.

Yasmin drew a literal representation of a metaphorical situation. Older children may feel more confident to paint their feelings in a more abstract way.

Zack was a talented twelve-year-old who was happy painting for most of the session. He sometimes asked for practical help but mostly he painted intently, quietly rebuffing any attempts by the therapist at conversation. The therapist bided her time, showing interest but not inquisitiveness. After three sessions, and when five pictures had been painted, Zack said he was ready to talk. The therapist asked whether he would display the paintings on a large easel and if she played the role of someone visiting an art gallery, whether he would play the role of a teacher explaining the pictures. He agreed readily. The pictures were mostly painted in red, purple and yellow and, speaking as the teacher, Zack explained that 'the artist was expressing his feelings of anger, hurt and joy in these pictures. This one represents the river of his life, bouncing over the rocks.'

This self-interpretation by Zack also shows how it is easier for a young person to speak of himself in the third person, as 'the artist'. Like Tim, who talked of 'the little boy', Zack found it less threatening to project his feelings onto another. The therapist should always respect this and stay within the projection until such time as the child feels it is safe to own the feelings. For a child who is unable to talk about personal matters this projection, or metaphor, can be initiated by the therapist. However, it is much more congruent if the child does this herself because the projection or metaphor may not be recognised if it is the creation of the therapist. If we listen carefully to stories or images which a child gives us, often at the first encounter, we can find something which will be apposite. One boy, for instance, told the story of Pinocchio during his first session. It was not developed at that time but during the next few sessions the therapist noticed that the issue of 'telling lies' was a major one. Pinocchio's nose, of course, grew longer whenever he told a lie. She was able to return to the theme of Pinocchio in future sessions and this enabled the boy to work through the difficulties he had suffered from adults who had lied about their abuse of him, and his own fears that he may have told lies about past events.

If a sandtray is available some children find this a satisfying way in which to play. I often carry a portable sandtray in a large plastic cake container. A small sandtray can also be made from a cat litter tray, half filled with sand. Boxes of plastic people, animals and fantasy characters are necessary for enactments in the sand. This kind of work was introduced by Margaret Lowenfeld (1979). Children are invited to play in the sand and then to tell the therapist what is going on. Children often enact complete psychodramas using the plastic characters and they can be encouraged to verbalise if necessary. Often, though, actions speak louder than words, as the medium of sand is conducive to digging, burying, leaving tracks and 'disappearing without trace'.

Zoe was only five when she came to therapy after physical abuse by her father. Her mother had left home two years previously, taking two older children. Zoe and her seven-year-old brother remained with dad, who was receiving separate therapy. After several sessions in which she had focused on the physical abuse, Zoe chose a female plastic doll and played in the sand, looking at the marks it left behind as she moved it about. After some time she buried it and smoothed it over. Then she placed a flag as a marker. 'The flag shows where you have buried her', remarked the therapist. 'Mm, nobody knows she's even been here', said Zoe. She gazed in silence at the sand and the marks previously left by the doll as she dragged it across the sand. 'She has been here though', she cried excitedly, 'you can see the marks'.

Later Zoe was able to talk freely about her mother, whom she had been forbidden to mention at home. She was able to grieve and to recognise the good things that her mother had given her, before she left home.

It is worth remembering that the sandtray provides containment of difficult or painful issues. A child like Zoe may find it impossible to talk about her mother, or to physically re-enact scenes where her mother was present. The sandtray, however, provides a small, well-boundaried area where a child can re-enact scenes and share feelings. For Zoe, who was not allowed to speak of mother at home, it was too dangerous to talk freely, even in the sessions. The metaphor and containment of the sandtray allowed her to express feelings. For her personal safety, it was important for her that 'her work' did not spill over into her everyday life. Allowing her to chose the sandtray was, therefore, essential for her.

THE DANGERS OF INTERPRETATION

As we saw with Zack and Zoe and with many of the other children, young people are closer to their unconscious feelings than most adults, and if they need an interpretation of their play they will supply one for themselves. I feel that it is important to let children know that I have heard what they have said, that I have noticed what they are feeling and that I can contain their anxieties safely. It is important that I mirror their feelings rather than supply an adult interpretation. Of course, this is precisely the same technique that Moreno used as he mirrored clients' situations to enable them to put things into perspective and to place some distance between their difficulties and themselves.

Therapists need to accept the chaos which their young clients present and allow them to find their own resolutions, with support from the workers. Winnicott stated that most children will eventually come up with their own interpretations and solutions and he felt that it was stealing their creativity to pre-empt this. When trauma enters our lives we merely exist and we cannot live as fully as we would wish. Our creativity is stifled at traumatic times but, with encouragement, it can grow and be used to heal the hurt. When this happens there is a great feeling of joy and satisfaction.

Children and adults often inadvertently use language which expresses their feelings more clearly than they realise. 'I don't know where I am', 'I'm all over the place', and 'I can't get myself together', all express feelings of dissociation, of splitting or projection which we all do when we are feeling distressed. Most children, especially younger ones, will frequently project their own feelings onto others and this is a normal developmental stage. It is helpful to encourage the child to own her feelings, but explaining to children that they are projecting their own feelings onto others is an unnecessary comment about behaviour which may be developmentally normal.

Young people who are moving between controlling and victimised behaviour are rehearsing roles for themselves, 'building themselves from roles', as Moreno said. Shakespeare knew this when he had the young Prince of Denmark utter these thoughts:

> To be or not to be: that is the question:
> Whether 'tis nobler in the mind to suffer
> The slings and arrows of outrageous fortune,
> Or to take arms against a sea of troubles,
> And by opposing end them?
>
> (Hamlet, Act III, Scene I)

This is the struggle which abused children have. Is it better to suffer one's fortune or to take arms against it? To be a victim or a controller. In Jungian terms, to allow the anima or animus to dominate. The therapist seeks to help the young person to find a creative, balanced solution wherein behaviour can be appropriate to the circumstance and not preordained because of past events.

WITNESSING THE PAIN

The notion of someone else knowing what happened or 'acting as a witness' for a child is a powerful one for those who have been abused. Older children often make comments to the therapist, such as 'I know you have seen what happened, I know you have heard me, and it makes me feel better.' Of course the therapist has seen and heard only the child's perception of what happened, but that is what is important. 'Finding the truth', or 'the facts' is not important from a therapeutic point of view, although, of course, in cases of abuse someone may need to investigate the evidence in order to protect the child.

Therapists who are not also skilled in investigating child abuse may find that they have to report information that a child may be suffering further abuse. If the information that the child gives is clear, or if there is physical evidence then, of course, there is no option but to report it so that it can be investigated. The proposed course of action should be explained carefully to the child and, if appropriate, to carers. Information which is ambiguous or which is only given within metaphor should be discussed thoroughly with a supervisor or colleague before any action is taken. Children should always be taken seriously and information they give should be carefully considered. In a criminal court, however, evidence has to be unequivocal. In a civil court, where proceedings might be taken to ensure the safety of a child, the evidence is based on the balance of probabilities. Proving that a child is being abused always takes the evidence of several professionals and other adults.

CHOICE AND EMPOWERMENT

The idea of following the child's agenda makes it obvious that a child should be given as much choice as possible when therapy is considered. Of course children usually have no idea what therapy means and they are almost always referred by an adult. (Some adolescents do refer themselves, however.) They must have the power to refuse therapy altogether and to refuse a particular therapist. Children's power to do this is limited and their experience of talking with people of different ages, gender and ethnic group may also be limited. Children with disability may have even narrower experience, perhaps because of lack of mobility. We should, therefore, be prepared to be as adaptable as possible and to ask for assistance from colleagues or other professionals if our own experience is limited to a particular ethnic group, gender or age group.

Giving children as much choice as possible regarding their therapist is as important as the choice of a suitable environment and play materials. Sometimes therapists can be over-enthusiastic about a particular kind of play equipment or method. Children who are coerced will seldom express their own thoughts and feelings.

Another area of choice concerns the length of sessions and the timing. Of course a therapist working for an organisation may be severely restricted regarding this. However, older children may be anxious about missing too many lessons at school, although it should also be borne in mind that a child who attends after school is likely to be tired. An hour is usually the maximum period for a session because concentration for both therapist and child is limited. For young children, however, twenty minutes or half an hour may be more suitable for a start.

THE IMPORTANCE OF CONTAINMENT

When Winnicott talked about the necessity of allowing the child to see that her anxiety can be contained within the therapeutic relationship, he was expressing the fear of children that they are omnipotent. They fear that their whole world is affected by their feelings and that if those feelings are so powerful then their whole world may be destroyed by them. A therapist must model her ability to contain her own emotions. Sometimes the pain of a child's hurt and humiliation is almost too much to bear, but bear it the therapist must if she is to help her client. To express the unspoken but obvious fear which a child has because his sexual abuser is still living in the same house, or in the same street, is to give some relief for the child, who learns that fear is a normal reaction to such a situation. To hold that fear, accepting it, whilst allowing the child to find some way of overcoming it, is to act as a truly therapeutic container. As we saw with Georgina in a previous chapter, once her fear was accepted and contained she soon found her own solution.

PROFESSIONAL SUPERVISION

One of the ways to contain all the feelings which are projected onto therapists by children is by having good, professional supervision for the therapists. When we face an onslaught of emotions and confused, powerful responses, which are projected onto us every day, we can begin to feel powerless, confused, helpless and chaotic. We feel, in fact, like the children we are trying to support. By having a supervisor whom we can trust, who is willing to hold up a mirror to our own confusions, we can contain our own emotions and we can ensure that we are not projecting those onto an already confused client.

To keep the boundaries for our clients we must make sure we know where our own boundaries are. We must not reflect and repeat the formless and uncontained lives which many abused children are forced to lead because their families are unable to 'hold things together'. The economic and psychological pressures upon many families are enormous; it is difficult for many to survive. For childcare workers too there are pressures of organisations as well as personal pressures and the stress of the work itself. We must be aware of when we are feeling unfit to work with children and be able to rely on our supervisors to tell us so, if we cannot see it ourselves.

5 WRITING, STORIES AND FAIRY STORIES: WITH INDIVIDUALS OR GROUPS

I am in a world of darkness,
A sufferer of pain,
My heart feels heavy, like a weight,
My body can take no more.
I feel tough, but I am weak,
And I am a survivor.

Rachel, aged twelve.

Writing, as creative expression and as therapy, has of course been used for centuries. As we saw in an earlier chapter, the child who survived the Aberfan disaster wrote about it, 'pages and pages'. Men and women have written journals, or even novels to extirpate the pain and suffering of traumatic events. It is a way of projecting the events, and the feelings, onto the page, and out of the body. As Rachel says, in the poem above, 'My body can take no more', so she places the pain within the poem.

There are many accounts of child sexual abuse by survivors who are now adults. Jacqueline Spring's *Cry Hard & Swim* (1987) was one of the first. Women and men are now realising how therapeutic it can be not only to place their feelings on the page but also to sort out and make sense of confused and ambiguous feelings.

A useful exercise for children who enjoy writing may be to write a letter to their abuser or to someone who failed to protect. The letter will never be sent but in writing it, and in sharing it with the therapist, the child has expressed the feelings and also had the feelings witnessed.

The use of stories

In *Playtherapy with Abused Children* (1992), Ann Cattanach, a dramatherapist, describes how she invites children to tell a story during her sessions with them. She describes a five-year-old boy who told a story about a bad-tempered crocodile 'whose dad made him eat willies'. Throughout the series of sessions the boy told a different story, often about the crocodile puppet with which he played. Each story expressed the difficulties which were facing him at that particular moment. Realistically, Ann states that the stories are likely to continue for some time.

Some children are reluctant to invent stories for themselves and prefer to be given a structure to contain them. Such a structure is described by dramatherapist Mooli Lahad (1992). He gives a six-part structure in which a child is invited to divide a piece of paper into six squares and write or draw a picture in each square in the manner of a comic book. Lahad also describes a way of using the story in an assessment of the child.

I have followed Lahad's method, adapting it slightly, and occasionally, if a child is suggesting that she would like to tell a story, but does not know where to start, I suggest the following steps:

1. Find a central character, person or animal and decide where they live.
2. Give them a task or a journey.
3. Decide whether there are any companions or helpers.
4. Who or what are the obstacles which your character encounters?
5. What happens next?
6. Does the story have an end?

Most stories contain these elements and the broad framework allows plenty of freedom for children to experiment. In fact a group can also use this structure to tell a composite story. The telling of a composite story probably works best with older children, from about eleven years. Children can co-operate well from about five years old but for some abused children this is more difficult. Generally I have restricted groups of abused children to eleven years and upwards and I keep the age range very narrow. From puberty the sexual knowledge of children varies greatly and although it is often assumed that sexually abused children have a wide sexual knowledge, this is not usually the case. Abused children are told

lies about sexuality by their perpetrators, often because the perpetrators themselves are ignorant, sometimes to enable the perpetrators to rationalise or justify what they do.

Sexually abused children fare best in small, single-gender
groups, with a ratio of one worker to three children. For girls,
female workers are usually chosen and for boys, one male and
one female is more appropriate. Many abused boys have been
abused by males, so the presence of two male workers would be
oppressive and most boys would feel safer with a woman there.
There are few, if any, groups for girls abused by women, but in
the same way one male and one female worker would provide
balance. Some older girls, at a later stage in their therapeutic
experience, can benefit from a male as well as a female worker.
The male can provide a good role model and may provide an
absolutely safe male on which the teenagers can project their
sexual fantasies. Of course the relationship between the therapists
must be open and unambiguous. It is unhelpful if there is a
sexual relationship because this repeats the parental pattern and
can cause problems for the young people.

Telling stories and sometimes acting them out can be helpful
for the young people in such groups. I have described elsewhere
(Bannister in Jennings 1995) the effectiveness of acting out a story
within a group. In this case the group asked to act out a court
scene and one of the young women took the part of the Judge. She
also took control of the story within the scene and described a
scenario which was similar to her own. The difference, of course,
was that she was able to be 'the Judge' rather than 'the Victim'. If
the group co-operate to tell a story which is, perhaps, symbolic of
their own experiences, it is more likely to benefit all members of
the group.

It should be remembered, however, that the group experience
of therapy ensures that 'common themes' recur frequently and a
story which seems to be devised by one member may well be
saying something important for other members. In psychodrama
this effect is well documented. A group which is not ready to
witness a particular kind of abusive behaviour will not choose to
follow the story of a member who they know, or sense, has
suffered in this way. On the other hand, when several members
are clamouring to act out their stories, it will often transpire
that they all have very similar themes and close connections,
and that the central figure in the story could have been any one
of the members who have asked for their story to be told and
witnessed.

A powerful effect of the group is that it can help its members to contain their difficulties, in a healthy way, until they, and the group, are ready to deal with them.

One young woman, Anna, had been in individual therapy for some time. When she joined the group and realised that psychodrama was being used she was keen to work on her abusive experiences within the group. For the first four weeks she offered to become the protagonist and to present her story to the group. Each time a different group member was chosen, in preference to her. On the fifth week Anna did not offer to work and the therapist judged that the group had been helping her to contain her story in a way which she had not been able to manage before. On the sixth week no one else came forward as a potential protagonist. Anna spoke up. 'I would like to do some work today. It's not about my abuse, it's about the future. I think I've been working on my abuse each time other group members have done their psychodramas. I am really pleased that I could do it. It makes a change for me not to be blurting everything out.' Anna went on to do an energetic and symbolic psychodrama of the future.

FAIRY STORIES

For centuries fairy stories have been told and because the same few themes and stories occur frequently throughout many parts of the world, writers have speculated on the uses of such stories in different cultures. Since such stories have been written down over the last three or four hundred years there is a chance to compare them and to note their amazing similarities. Whilst talking about the use of fairy tales with groups of adult women who have been sexually abused, some have expressed surprise that I would use stories that seem to keep girls and women in their place, stories which may promise a happy ending for the Heroine who is rescued by the Prince. Perhaps I am interested in the fact that the tellers of fairy stories in most cultures have traditionally been women and that these folk tales have often been denigrated, discounted and disbelieved. A fairly cursory look at the history of fairy tales soon shows us that fairy stories change quite radically when they are written down by male writers such as the Brothers Grimm.

The story of Cinderella appears in an Egyptian version and a Chinese version as well as in most European countries. Cinderella does not simply wait for 'her Prince to come' in most of the stories. The sanitised Disney version with her golden hair is not recognisable in the resourceful daughter, grieving for her dead mother, who escapes the tyranny of her family and finds the happiness she seeks.

In *The Uses of Enchantment* Bruno Bettelheim (1976) uses the developmental idea of 'splitting' to explain how a child may use a fairy story to split off the 'good' and 'bad' parts of the mother into 'Fairy Godmother' and 'Wicked Stepmother'. For children who are having difficulty in integrating the two sides of their own or their mother's personality, this split can help them to hold the two separate until they are ready to make the integration.

I believe that children are attracted to fairy tales because they recognise the struggle for acceptance which the central character always faces. The personal qualities of the hero/heroine are seldom appreciated by those around them. They may have a long and difficult journey or task to complete before they win through. There are usually some friends (often animals) who act as helpers and companions. In the end they do win through and this is not just to show the triumph of good over evil (although this may be satisfying for many children), but it shows the listening child that others have struggled and wept and been misunderstood, and yet they have succeeded.

The maxim of always 'following the child's agenda' holds good in the telling of fairy tales. We cannot know which story holds most meaning for a child at a particular time. Recently I saw a small boy whose home life had been temporarily shattered.

Aaron was five years old and he was in a temporary foster home with his nine-year-old brother whilst his father was hospitalised. Both boys had lived with their father for some years since their parents' marriage had failed. Aaron picked up the farm animals in the therapy room and separated them all carefully into families. All the sheep were herded together, likewise the cows and pigs and, placing them on a large sheet of paper, he drew fences with cray-ons to contain them all neatly. He looked at the piglets and said, 'Do you know a story about three little pigs?' I nodded and asked if he would like to tell me the story. 'You tell it to me', he said, making himself comfortable on a floor cushion, where we were sitting. I began the story and Aaron joined in at the parts he liked. 'Little pig, little pig, let me in, let me in', he chanted with me, as the wolf. 'No, by the hair of my chinny chin chin, I will not let you in', he squealed delightedly as the little pig. 'Then I'll huff and I'll puff and I'll blow your house down', we both roared. 'And the

wolf gobbled up the little pig ...' I continued, keeping to the origi-
nal story. 'No', corrected Aaron. 'He went to live with his brother
for a bit.' I realised that Aaron had probably been told a modern
version where the two little pigs were not eaten by the wolf.
'Right', I said, 'So the next little pig built a house of sticks ....'

Bettelheim considers that the original story of the three little pigs
is acceptable for children because they recognise that each pig
represents a stage of a child's life and so each pig can die, just as a
stage of life finishes, because at the end the biggest pig, who represents the young adult, triumphs over the wolf. I tend to agree with
this but at the same time I always go along with the child's
corrections or changes because he must put his own meaning on
the story.

After the wolf had blown down the house of sticks Aaron told me
that both pigs went to their big brother who was building a house
of bricks. He invited me to continue the story until we came to
the part where the wolf could not blow down the house of bricks.
Excitedly, he took over completely and described the big pot of
boiling water that the pig placed on the fire to catch the wolf who
was climbing down the chimney. 'And ... Splash! ... he was burned
and was all dead', he said, with relish, 'and the little pigs lived
happily ever after'.

So the gruesome death at the end of the story apparently caused
Aaron no problems. Aaron's house of straw had been blown down
when his parents split up. His house of sticks was also blown down
when his father was taken into hospital because of long-standing
mental health problems. Aaron probably recognised that this house
was unlikely to be rebuilt. He looked to his older brother, or to his
more grown-up self, to build a more enduring house.

  The beauty of fairy stories is that they can be changed by each
child to suit the circumstances. The original form endures, some
changes are absorbed into the fabric of the story, others are transi-
tory, existing only for an individual child.

Bridie was thrilled with the scraps of material and the hats and
'crowns' that constituted the dressing-up box. She wrapped a piece
of veiling around her and placed a crown on her head. 'I'm Cin-
derella', she said, 'going to the ball'. Bridie was thirteen and had
been abused by several men in her family. She felt she was 'fat
and ugly'. She danced dreamily to imaginary music. 'I'm waiting,'

she said, 'waiting for Mat to come'. 'Mat?' queried the therapist,
wondering what happened to the Prince. 'Mat!' Bridie replied,
impatiently, 'Mat from Bros.' Bros was a pop group and, like other
girls of her age, Bridie had turned one of its members into her very
own 'Prince'.

The story of Cinderella satisfies children of both sexes as they
recognise that the adolescent child may be fulfilled by a pairing
with another person, other than a parent. The story is undoubtedly
sexual, the symbol of the shoe which fits perfectly reminds us of
that, and to an adolescent the sexuality is its main impact. To a
younger child the awareness of sibling rivalry as the Ugly Sisters
issue their commands, may be more important.

As we shall see in chapter 7 it may be important when working
with children from different cultures to find out how these universal stories have been told in their own communities.

Of course the therapists for Aaron and Bridie did not explain
the meaning of the stories to them. Such explanations may be
helpful for the therapist but children are merely using the story as
a framework which is useful to separate and sort out the chaos of
their lives. Just as Aaron, in the previous example, drew fences to
separate all the different parts of his life, so the story helps children to keep 'good' and 'bad' apart until they are able to integrate
the two parts, both of the self, and of others. Abused children
often suffer chaotic, confused lives and even when children are
given careful explanations these are not always absorbed because
there is too much turmoil. A fairy story, on the other hand, can be
repeated endlessly, so that children can learn the framework for
themselves and can call on it whenever necessary. Children often
say, 'No one has told me anything', when asked if they have
received an explanation after a traumatic event. Sometimes this is
absolutely true but sometimes people have tried to tell but the
child is unable to listen. Most of us can identify with the difficulty
of 'hearing' when we are worried. Studies have shown that patients
often remember only a very small part of a doctor's instructions
after a consultation. Children often have better memories than
adults but they may not understand what has been said, and explanations are often full of adult-centred expressions. Naturally it is
still important to give careful factual explanations to children
whose lives are in chaos but it is also important to give them the
possibility of understanding through the medium of stories.

The violence in fairy stories has been condemned but I
believe that because these stories are so obviously fantasy, and

are about Kings and Queens or dragons and other creatures, children know that the violence is also symbolic. Bettelheim quotes a study of ten-year-olds, some of whom had a rich fantasy life through stimulation with fairy stories, who were exposed to a film with a violent content. The children with the knowledge and exposure to fairy stories showed a decrease in aggressive behaviour after seeing the film, whereas the other children, described as 'low-fantasy' children, showed an increase (Biblow in Singer 1973, quoted in Bettelheim 1976). Of course there may have been other factors in the lives of the children which also affected their reactions.

Some modern writers have successfully faced the accusation that girls and women are passive creatures in fairy stories, who wait to be rescued, by boys or men. Angela Carter, who edited the *Virago Book of Fairy Tales* (Carter 1990), gathers, from all over the world, stories which all have a female as the protagonist. She has not changed the stories; she points out that they were already there and have survived in the verbal tradition. The stories she has collected are often bawdy and it is easy to see how they may have been repressed, along with female sexuality, during patriarchal and puritan periods. They are also stories of brave and resourceful girls and clever women and they cover cultures from India to Africa and America. The similarities are striking.

Marina Warner (1994) in her book on fairy tales and their tellers reminds us that when men and women tell the same tale they frequently give it a different emphasis. Women often emphasise the co-operation of the women in the stories and their courage and determination. Men sometimes emphasise the importance of lineage or the acquisition of treasure. She points out, however, that both sexes frequently tell tales of ineffective men and wicked women, as in *Cinderella* and *Snow White*. This tendency is repeated today in TV 'soaps' such as *Coronation Street* and *Last of the Summer Wine*. Childlike men are organised by contemptuous women.

Many abused children feel angry with one or both parents who, they feel, should have protected them from abuse. If one parent is abusive then the child's anger is often directed at the other parent, especially if this is a mother. Somehow all the anger, humiliation and powerlessness is projected onto the mother, who may be a victim of abuse herself, either from her partner or from her original family. To express this anger can be dangerous for a child who fears that if she does so she will then lose her last vestiges of protection. The therapist can help a child to do this by using a psychodramatic technique which splits the good mother from the bad mother. Of course this is the same technique which a fairy story uses as it splits off the 'real mother' who is often dead, from the 'wicked stepmother' who is so cruel and unprotective.

Chris felt that his mother should have protected him from his father who had sexually abused him from the age of seven to eleven. He had tried to tell her about the abuse but she had not listened or believed him. She had suggested that he had misunderstood his father's behaviour and Chris was furious that he had been further abused before she finally believed what he was saying. The therapist used the technique of 'the empty chair' and asked Chris if he wanted to bring his mother into the chair to tell her his feelings. He agreed eagerly and began to tell her how angry he felt. His voice rose and tears were near the surface as he shouted 'Why didn't you listen to me?' He picked up a bataka which was lying in the therapy room. (A bataka is a stick which can be made from tightly rolled newspaper or foam and wrapped around with sticky tape to make it firm.) As he lifted the bataka the tears ran down his cheeks. 'I can't hit her', he said, 'she's my mum'. The therapist asked Chris what were the good things about his mother that he wished to protect. He talked about her playfulness when she took him to the park and they both rode on the swings. He remembered his favourite food which she sometimes cooked for him and he smiled as he told the therapist of the stories his mother used to tell him at bedtime when he was smaller. 'Let's make sure we keep all those bits safe', said the therapist and Chris carefully took the precious qualities of his mother and placed them on another chair. 'Now they are safe', said the therapist, 'you can't destroy those. What about what's left?' The bataka came down with a thwack on the empty chair. 'It was wicked, wicked, wicked,' shouted Chris. 'Why didn't you believe me?' He went on to tell the bad part of his mother how angry he was and how specifically she had ignored him or not listened to him. Then he moved over to the chair containing the 'good mother' and he placed his head on the seat as if he was placing it on her lap. Later the therapist was able to set up a session for Chris and his mother to talk honestly about their feelings.

It is not necessary, when using this technique, to refer to fairy stories at all but perhaps a knowledge of fairy tales helps a child to understand the notion of the good and bad split. Some children are more explicit, such as thirteen-year-old Danielle.

*'The story of my life!', exclaimed Danielle as she picked up a book containing the story of Beauty and the Beast. The therapist waited for an explanation, raising her eyebrows in an unspoken question. 'Not that I think I'm beautiful', Danielle continued, smoothing her long fair hair with her hand, 'but **he** was certainly a Beast'. Danielle's mother had been addicted to drugs and found it difficult to bring up her child alone. The 'Wicked Fairies', represented by the social workers in this case, had compelled Danielle's mother to 'abandon' her and she had spent the years between three and nine in a series of foster homes. From the age of seven she had been physically and sexually abused by a foster father until the social workers, now transformed into 'Good Fairies', had again removed her. This time she found herself in a very supportive foster home where the foster parents, and their extended family, were helping Danielle to recover from her early traumas. She had asked to go to therapy, with her foster parents' support, 'to finally sort out what happened'. Putting her own interpretation on the fairy story, Danielle told the therapist that she had often felt like the Beauty in the story when she was a little girl. She mourned her mother, whom she loved, and blamed others for taking her away. She said she felt truly abandoned when the Beast began to abuse her. 'And that Beast did not turn into a beautiful Prince', confirmed the therapist. 'No', said Danielle, 'But I know that all men are not beasts now.'*

Danielle's new family, and perhaps the therapist herself, had helped Danielle to recover from a horrific experience. Danielle had placed her own story within the context of the fairy story and had given herself hope and on the way she had acquired wisdom and courage. Perhaps Hope, Wisdom and Courage were the Good Fairies who were present at her Christening, as in all the best fairy stories, along with the Wicked Fairy. Or perhaps Danielle, using the fantasy-rich life which someone (perhaps her mother) had given her, was able to find these qualities for herself. In time she may also recognise the 'Wicked Fairy' qualities within herself and be able to relieve herself of much guilt and pain.

Danielle, at thirteen, and having had some individual therapy, was able to move on to join a group for adolescent girls who had been sexually abused. The young women in such groups may be invited to tell stories and to enact them in fantastic ways to facilitate their expression of feelings about their experiences. In one group of older teenage girls (most of whom were mothers themselves) there had been sessions which included drawing and painting, followed by a 'gallery' when paintings were shown to each other so that their feelings could be witnessed. The young women did not have to share the meaning of the paintings, although they often chose to do so. It was enough that their feelings had been witnessed by others. After the painting session, and the gallery, several young women shared the deep humiliation of their abusive experience. There was relief and even some laughter in the sharing of the actual feelings of their experience, as opposed to the sharing of the facts.

One young woman, Ellie, suggested, 'Let's give the bastards a taste of their own medicine. Let's do a story where they get what's coming to them.' Since there had already been sessions where the group had thrown clay at pictures or symbols of their abusers which they had pinned to the wall, the two co-therapists wondered what might transpire. Already they had kicked cushions and torn boxes to express anger. They had shouted and stamped to music and made their own music with drums and cymbals. But the therapists had forgotten the fairy stories where the evil one is forced to suffer in the same way as the victim. In some versions of Bluebeard, for instance, the Bride locks him in the same cellar as his former bridal victims, and he perishes alongside the corpses.

The group found a battered old teddy bear to represent all their abusers and they held a 'psychodramatic party'. They plied the old bear with drink whilst dancing round pretending they were drunk themselves. When teddy passed out they laid him on 'a bed' and shackled his hands and feet to the bedposts. The therapists could almost 'see' the fairytale four-poster on which the villain was spreadeagled, naked. The group danced round him, like witches round a cauldron. They draped his genital area with a piece of tinsel left over from the recent group Christmas party. 'Let's 'phone the ...' said Ellie, naming a popular daily paper and scandal sheet. 'We have a famous MP here', she said into the imaginary telephone, whilst the other girls giggled encouragingly. 'Send a photographer to see what he gets up to in his spare time.' The group disappeared to the edges of the room and asked a therapist to play the photographer whilst they looked on. They had stopped giggling. This was serious. 'Let's hope all his friends see the picture in the papers', said one. 'What friends?' asked Ellie.

The humiliation of the abuser, which reflected their own humiliation, was complete. I believe also that this less aggressive way of dealing with anger often feels more appropriate for many young women.

The connection with incestuous sexual abuse and fairy stories
or myths is explicit, most obviously in the Oedipal myth and
also in the many variations of the Donkey Skin story. In this
story the Princess's mother is dying. The King is distraught and
on her deathbed the Queen asks him not to marry again unless
he can find a bride as beautiful as she. The Queen dies and the
King, realising that his daughter is the only woman as beautiful
as the Queen, asks her to become his wife. She refuses and sets
him impossible tasks, which he manages to perform, so she
hides herself in a stinking donkey skin and escapes from the
castle. After many trials and tribulations she meets her Prince,
who recognises that she is a Princess and marries her. Warner
suggests that this story is probably connected to the story known
as 'the She-Bear' where another widowed King decides to take his
daughter as his wife. In desperation she goes to her old nurse
who gives her a stick which, if she puts it into her mouth when
her father comes to her room, will turn her into a bear, so that
she can run away.

I feel that these stories are describing the coping mechanism of
dissociation which many children learn to use when they are being
abused or hurt in any way. Many of us are familiar with the idea
of 'stepping outside oneself', or 'becoming separate from the body'
so that the pain which is perpetrated on the body is hardly felt
because the 'real person' is not in it. This coping mechanism has
been discussed in chapters 2 and 3.

A child who is being abused may 'become' a bear, or a donkey,
or even the flower on the wallpaper, in order to bear the extreme
pain, humiliation and terror which is present whilst the abuse is
taking place. After months or years of doing this deliberately a
child may find that the dissociation is involuntary and she has lost
control of the mechanism, which then becomes dysfunctional. Of
course it may have already caused serious difficulties for the child
because if she is dissociating she may be unable to absorb school
work or listen to instructions. It is possible that a fairy story can
help a child to recognise what she is doing or, more likely, after
the abuse has been discovered, the story could help her to release
herself from the Bear or the Donkey Skin and find her own personality. Warner points out that these stories of incest have been
repressed or altered after the eighteenth century. It may be that a
well-meaning 'cleaning up' of fairy tales has actually damaged the
way in which they can help children to cope with life's difficulties.
The disappearance of the incest motif from popular tales (although
it remained in classical myth) may have added to the disbelief

which was suffered by most sexually abused children during the nineteenth and most of the twentieth century.

There is even a connection between sexual abuse and mental illness which is enshrined in the story of St Dympna, from the thirteenth century. She refused the sexual advances of her father and escaped, with her companions, to exile. Her father eventually caught up with her and killed her. Dympna has become the patron saint of the mentally ill, perhaps in recognition that a child who is burdened with a sexually abusive father is bound to be seriously affected, whether or not she is able to escape from him. This may also reflect the knowledge that the physical part of sexual abuse is not necessarily the part which causes the damage. It is the over-whelming abuse of power which destroys.

One of the most entertaining storytellers I have met is a drama-therapist named Alida Gersie. Her book *Earthtales* (1992) chroni-cles some of her stories and also gives good advice on the running of groups. She also makes suggestions for group activities which follow the telling of stories by the group leader. For those who have a very wide knowledge of stories this is a useful way to work because all the stories have universal themes and there will always be something in a story for a few of the group members to work on. The stories are suitable for adults as well as children. Alida also works with group members to create their own stories as I do.

It is important, however, that therapists do not try to transpose what is suitable for a group onto a session with an individual child. A group therapist who is in tune with the mood of the group may well find a story each week that resonates with at least some of the group members. It is much less likely that this will happen with a therapist and an individual child (although occasionally it does so). The therapist who wishes to use stories may tell short stories to a child in order to increase that child's knowledge of stories. We should not, however, expect the stories which we choose to have immediate meaning or effect on the child. The effect is much more likely to be observed when a child has initiated a story himself. In the following example, however, the therapist did tell a story, which was prompted by a picture which the child had painted. Because he was in an ongoing relationship with the therapist she felt able to introduce a story which she felt would have some meaning for him.

Twelve-year-old Fintan enjoyed painting and enjoyed showing his therapist how he could paint a butterfly by painting one wing and folding the paper over to make a matching imprint on the other side. The butterfly was very colourful and beautiful. Underneath, Fintan painted a large, brown, worm-like creature. The therapist watched quietly whilst the painting progressed. 'Are you anywhere in this picture?', she asked. Fintan replied quickly, pointing to the worm, 'That's me', he said. 'I'm a cocoon.' The therapist asked about a 'cocoon' and Fintan explained that it started as a caterpillar and 'covered itself with all this brown and green stuff which got hard'.

It felt important for the therapist not to rush into using this material. Fintan had been multiply abused by several members of his family, and extended family, for the first seven years of his life. The therapist reflected that sometimes, in therapy, it had seemed that he was as hard and dry as a chrysalis and that he was difficult to reach. She remembered the story of the Lingworm, an old folk tale, and at his next session she asked him if he would like to hear it. He said he would and this is the story:

Once upon a time, in a country far away, lived a beautiful Queen who was sad because she had no children. One day, whilst walking in the wood, she met an old, wise woman. 'Why are you so sad?' asked the old crone. 'I would like to have a child', replied the Queen. 'When you walk in the wood tomorrow you will see a bush bearing a beautiful red rose and a beautiful white rose. Pick the red and you will have a boy child, pick the white and the child will be a girl. But remember, on no account pick them both.'

The next day the Queen saw the rose bush, as promised, but the flowers were so beautiful she could not resist picking them both. Shortly afterwards the King announced that he must go off to the war and would not return for several months. While he was away the Queen took to her bed and, with her servants in attendance, she gave birth. First of all she gave birth to a large, brown Lingworm which slithered away and escaped, much to the relief of the servants. Immediately afterwards a beautiful Prince was born and the Queen asked the servants not to tell anyone about the Lingworm.

The King arrived home and was overjoyed with his baby son. He grew to be a handsome young Prince and one day he told his father that he was going to seek a Princess for his bride. As he journeyed he came to a crossroads where he met a huge, brown Lingworm. 'Where are you going?' asked the Worm. 'To find a Princess to make her my bride', answered the Prince. 'You cannot do that', replied the Lingworm. 'I am your brother and I am the

eldest. It is the law of the country that I must find a bride first
before you can marry.' The Prince returned at once to the Castle
and told the Queen who admitted that the Lingworm was speaking
the truth. The King declared that he would ask for a girl to marry
the Lingworm and he would give them both half his Kingdom. A
young girl came forward, pushed by her greedy father, and the
wedding took place. The morning after the wedding, when the
servants entered the bridal chamber they found the Lingworm look-
ing very full, with a few drops of blood on his face. Of the girl
there was no trace.

In despair the King asked for another girl to marry the Ling-
worm and, yet again, a greedy father presented his poor, frightened
daughter to the Lingworm. Once again the poor girl disappeared
and no one could be sure that the marriage had truly been
celebrated.

The King's woodcutter had a beautiful daughter. 'I am too old
to cut wood now', he said to her. 'If you marry the Lingworm we
will both have riches and I will have a happy old age.' The girl,
who loved her father, walked into the wood and cried because she
knew she must obey him. She met an old, wise woman who
advised her to go through the marriage ceremony with the Ling-
worm but to dress herself in seven white shifts when they retired
to the bridal chamber. She also advised her to take a bowl of water
and a bowl of milk into the room.

The poor girl did as she was bidden and after the ceremony
asked the servants to bring the milk and water. She put on the
seven white shifts and awaited the Lingworm. 'Remove your shift',
he declared as he entered the room. 'I will remove my shift if you
will remove a skin', she replied. 'But it will hurt', said the Ling-
worm, surprised by her request. 'I will wash you tenderly and
bathe you in milk', she said. The Lingworm reluctantly agreed.
Throughout the night the Lingworm repeated his request because,
of course, there were seven shifts to be removed. Each time she
removed a shift, he removed a skin and gently she cared for him
and eased his pain.

The next morning the servants entered the chamber in fear,
expecting the girl to have disappeared. To their amazement the
girl sat up in the bed, smiling. By her side was a beautiful
young Prince. The King and Queen and the whole Kingdom
rejoiced and the other brother found his Princess and all of them
lived happily ever after.

After the story had finished Fintan nodded quietly. 'I think I
will have to start shedding my skins', he said. In subsequent

sessions Fintan worked hard, with the therapist, recalling painful feelings connected with the abuse, and expressing some of his anger and hurt. Sometimes it was just too difficult for him to continue the work but over the weeks he managed to release many of the feelings which had been locked inside for so long. The final session consisted of Fintan and the therapist flying around as butterflies. This rapidly changed to aeroplanes and Fintan talked about his hopes for the future.

Television programmes and films often take the place of fairy stories and myths in the lives of some children. Cult films, television shows and aggressively marketed toys thrust themselves into the child's world. Sometimes there is remarkably little effect on the children but if they do seem to be obsessed or fascinated by a particular film or toy it is always worth exploring this. It is unlikely that the obsession is simply that the commodity is well-marketed. It is more possible that the item has a special meaning for that child.

Some time ago, when Transformers were the latest toys for children, Francis, aged seven, came to his therapy session clutching a toy car which transformed itself into a figure of a man. He ran around the room, picking up toys and asking if they could all change into something else. When told that the other toys could not change he said, 'They could if I had a magic wand though.' Francis was using an idea from fairy stories, that things can change with a bit of magic, and he was including the modern idea of Transformer toys within that notion. The therapist went along with his idea and together they practised. They changed a small table into a boat by turning it upside down and sitting in it. They changed a baby doll into a fairy by giving her a magic wand. Francis was wondering if he dare change his behaviour. The angry feelings which had precipitated his temper tantrums had dissipated as his therapy progressed and his mother had received advice on how to handle the outbursts. The tantrums had achieved their object, however, so he was reluctant to give them up entirely. After all, his mother had given him plenty of attention. He picked up the baby doll, now a fairy, and waved it over his head. 'She is magicking me', he explained, 'I'm a Transformer.' Francis stopped having tantrums when his own 'transformation scene' was accomplished.

Both Fintan and Francis recognised the need for some transformation, for themselves as well as for others. Each boy symbolised his struggle in a way which was most meaningful for him. The therapist can only follow the child's route, but she brings her skills and creativity to the journey and, most of all, she gives support and encouragement.

In this chapter we have looked at writing, stories and fairy stories and, along the way, we have discussed the effectiveness of group work as well as individual therapy. I am sometimes also asked to work with sibling groups and at one time it seemed a good idea to me to see two to four siblings all together. However, it soon became apparent that for abused children this was not very useful. Each child needed individual attention and the strong family patterns persisted in the group and resisted change. I have found it more fruitful to see that each child has individual therapy and, when they are ready, and aware of their own strength and power, then they can meet together. It is most effective if two therapists work individually with all the siblings then, when the sibling group meets, the two therapists can run the group sessions.

One of the most difficult situations is where one brother or sister abuses another and in the next chapter we will look at children who sexually abuse other children and the different style of approach which is necessary.

6   CHILDREN WHO ABUSE OTHERS

The Queen turned crimson with fury, and, after glaring at her for a moment like a wild beast, screamed 'Off with her head'.

from *Alice's Adventures in Wonderland*, by Lewis Carroll

As we discussed in chapter 3 children cope with their own difficult or traumatic experiences in a variety of ways. Most children experiment with different coping behaviours until they find a mode which fits in with their life. Children can swing between extremely passive and very controlling behaviours, at least until seven or eight years old. Most children of this age will not have learned that sexual behaviour can be used as a weapon, unless they have been sexually abused themselves. Between the ages of three and five, sexual curiosity about themselves and others is normal behaviour but as children become socialised, usually on attending school, then this mutual exploratory behaviour becomes less common. The exception to this is group sexual behaviour, which may be initiated, in the form of a game, by a child who has had a sexually abusive experience. Peer pressure means that many children may join in the game, just as bullying behaviour can also be encouraged by one or more children who have been physically or emotionally abused.

ADULT SEXUAL ABUSERS

In adolescence, of course, sexual exploration is common, and normal, but this is also the age when most adult perpetrators of sexual abuse say that they started abusing. Various studies of adult and adolescent sexual offenders (such as Freeman-Longo 1982) have shown that a third to a half declare that they were sexually abused in childhood but around three-quarters say they were physically abused. Emotional abuse and neglect are, perhaps, more difficult to quantify but from my own work with sexual offenders I would say that this was a feature in them all. However, as Alice

Miller points out, most people accept a degree of emotional abuse in their childhood and fail to recognise their experience as abusive. If they then repeat this behaviour onto their own or other children they may rationalise it by declaring that it is 'for the child's good' and that 'it has not done me any harm'.

One man, who had repeatedly been jailed for sexual abuse offences against children, told his treatment group that he had 'never been abused' as a child. The remaining members of the group, all prisoners for similar offences, looked disbelieving since they had all been able to talk about their own physical or sexual abuse. The man then began to boast about the 'freedom' he had been given as a child. As he talked more it was clear that from a very early age he had been forced to scavenge the streets and rely on the generosity of neighbours for food. He had seldom been disciplined for aggressive or dishonest behaviour because his parents were hardly ever at home. When he did see them they seriously physically abused him but he described that as 'fair punishment' for all his misdemeanours. It was some time before he was able to understand that his own childhood had been abusive and to connect this with his own abusing behaviour.

Of course, most abused children do not go on to sexually abuse others. Adolescent and adult sexual abuse perpetrators gain some sexual satisfaction from abusing. Many abusers in treatment deny this initially, especially in incest cases, but eventually most admit that this is so. Pre-pubertal children probably do not receive sexual satisfaction and the main gratification in the behaviour is undoubtedly the control and power which is gained. It is not difficult to see why children (who lack power in an adult world) become doubly disempowered if they are abused in any way and so the idea of taking power over another child is born. Control and power are, therefore, at the heart of sexually abusive behaviour and after adolescence sexual gratification helps to make the behaviour addictive.

David Finkelhor (1984) suggested that there were four preconditions which were necessary before an adult abused a child. These conditions related to:

• Motivation

• Internal inhibitors

• External inhibitors

• The victim's resistance.

As we have seen, the motivation in an adult may be sexual gratification. It may also be an emotional congruence to children and a blockage in adult relationships. For a child abuser this motivation is usually power and control.

Internal inhibitors should be developed in an adult and in an abuser they may be lessened by the use of alcohol or substances. The adult also may have been abused and his empathic responses have been suppressed in order to cope with his own abuse. Although some child abusers deliberately use alcohol or substances to lower inhibitions, many may never have learned sexual inhibitions and, of course, most will have their own empathic responses repressed because of their own abuse.

The external inhibitors which an adult abuser has to face are usually the presence of a protective parent figure but these are overcome when there is an absence of a protector or there are particular opportunities for an abuser to be alone with a child. Similarly, a child abuser can be given unacceptable responsibilities in caring for a younger sibling and be charged with responsibilities which are not actually his.

The final factor in Finkelhor's preconditions is the resistance of the child victim and this is exactly the same whether the abuser is an adult or another child. The victim child may be emotionally insecure, have little knowledge of sexual matters or have a disability. There are thus many opportunities for coercion.

Modern treatment for adult sexual abusers concentrates, therefore, on breaking or controlling the addictive cycle of behaviour, initiating more acceptable reactions by solving nonsexual problems in nonsexual ways and by seeking support from friends and relatives. This kind of programme has many parallels with modern treatment for other addictions such as alcohol and drug misuse.

Before this kind of treatment programme was introduced, sexual offenders were either not treated at all or were treated psychotherapeutically, without the behavioural work. The treatment was based on an understanding of intrapsychic theory, based on Freud's concepts. Although this theory has helped us to understand sexuality, the treatment based on it had very limited success, as did more radical treatment such as chemical castration or the use of libido-reducing drugs. More recently, psychotherapeutic work on the abuser's own trauma has been introduced as part of a planned treatment programme, after the behavioural work is completed, or well under way. This work can include cognitive therapy, helping the offender to understand how his understanding and beliefs have been distorted, often by those who have been the perpetrators of trauma against him. Clinicians have begun to realise that treatment is more complete if this psychotherapy is included. However, since many perpetrators of abuse begin offending in early adolescence, or even before, and treatment may not be started for twenty or thirty years, success rates are not high. The addictive behaviour will have continued for so long that it is much harder for this cycle to be broken. The behaviour is, therefore, treatable, but in adults it is not necessarily curable. The philosophy of this kind of treatment is described by Anna Salter in *Treating Child Sex Offenders and Victims* (Salter 1988).

ADOLESCENT SEXUAL ABUSERS

In the early 1980s professionals began to recognise that if preventative work was to be done with sexual abusers then it was better to start as soon as possible, before the offending behaviour became entrenched. Research was beginning to confirm that sexually abusive behaviour starts at adolescence or earlier (Abel et al. 1985) and so treatment programmes for adolescents sprang up in the US and, later, in Britain. Researchers in the US had found that there had been a tendency (which was later confirmed in Britain) for courts or police to reduce charges of sexual assault against young people to lesser offences in the mistaken belief that young people would 'grow out of it' (Ryan in Ryan & Lane 1991).

On the contrary, this misguided policy only confirmed the offending behaviour and also effectively prevented adolescents from getting any help with their deviant behaviour, which was effectively dismissed, with a 'boys will be boys' attitude or disbelieved, especially when the offender was a girl. Under-reporting added to the problem and when young people were eventually charged with sexual offences there were often many different types of offence and the offender had received no help or treatment.

When treatment programmes were set up it was realised that adolescents, who are very influenced by their peers, would respond to group treatment which used peer pressure and which also educated the young people in human sexuality, social values, social skills, problem solving, anger management, victim awareness and also, perhaps, some psychotherapy to work on the offender's own traumatic experiences. Many programmes also used family therapy. Psychodrama was used in many programmes in the US to explore several of the areas mentioned, especially sexuality and relationships and to practice such skills as problem solving.

This treatment work with adolescents helped to develop an understanding of the sexual abuse cycle (Lane in Ryan & Lane 1991). The sexual abuse cycle is a description of the process which is deemed to occur before, during and after a sexual offence. The cyclical nature ensures that each offence reinforces the pattern of behaviour which is very difficult to change. Sandy Lane, who conceived the idea of the cycle, states that at first the young person is responding to feelings of helplessness and vulnerability. In other words, the initial response is based on a victim stance. He has negative expectations, believing that 'the worst will happen'. At first he attempts to 'avoid trouble', perhaps by trying unsuccessfully to avoid the person or people who are abusing him. When this is not possible he then moves to controlling behaviour with others who are more vulnerable than himself. It is at this point that his behaviour may become sexualised. He may have fantasies of sexual control, which may be reinforced by masturbation and this may lead to actual sexual assault. After the assault there is fear of getting caught and this leads to denial, rationalisation and minimisation in an effort to compensate. This angry response feeds into the familiar negative expectations of the victim response. So the cyclical behaviour continues. I have simplified and adapted Sandy Lane's original concept in Figure 6.1.

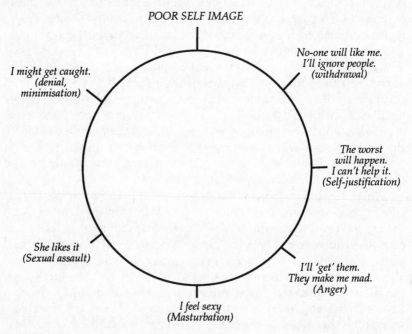

Figure 6.1 The cycle of abusive behaviour

ASSESSMENT: EXPLORATION, EXPLOITATION OR EXPERIMENTATION?

Before we consider treatment for a child who appears to be sexually abusing others, we must assess whether the behaviour is actually exploitation or whether it is normal exploration. Sexually exploitative behaviour may be noticed in children as young as five or six. Traditionally, this behaviour has been either ignored or severely punished. Children have had no opportunity to understand their behaviour, since their attempts to do so have been repressed. A recent piece of research in the area found a great reluctance on the part of professionals (social workers in this case), parents and the children themselves, to admit that the behaviour had any significance (Bannister & Gallagher 1995 and 1997).

It is difficult, therefore, for a proper assessment to be made. Is the child's motivation simply curiosity or, more worrying, is the child experimenting with behaviour which has been witnessed or in which this child was the victim? Curiosity is a likely explanation in children up to the age of five or six and simple education about body parts will usually be sufficient to stop the behaviour. Children of six to ten can also be heavily influenced by the pressure of their friends and if the sexualised behaviour is taking place in the form of a group game the motivation may also be without sinister implications. In sexual behaviour post-puberty, of course, when sexual drives may be high, the issues of consent need to be explored carefully.

It may be useful for adults who are worried about the sexual behaviour of a child to ask questions such as those devised by Print and Dey (in Bannister 1992: 111) to ascertain the motivation. They suggest the following:

- Why has the child's behaviour caused concern, and to whom?

- What preceded the behaviour, was it planned or spontaneous?

- Was the behaviour age inappropriate?

- In what context did the behaviour occur?

- Did the other child give informed and true consent?

- Was the behaviour persistent? Has the abuser been confronted about his behaviour previously?

- What was the power differential between the children involved?

- Were overt aggression or threats used?

- Did the child attempt to ensure secrecy?

- What was the experience of and effects on the recovering child?

- What was the abusing child's reaction to what occurred?

As I have already discussed, there are many 'normal' developmental reasons why some children may exhibit behaviour which appears to be sexually abusing. It will be seen from this list that attention must also be paid to the motivation and cultural expectations of the adult who is concerned about the abuse. In some cultures sexual curiosity, even in young children, may be discouraged. In other cultures masturbation, for instance, may be encouraged in young children as a form of comfort and the child may merely be inappropriately masturbating in front of others. A simple instruction from parents or teachers may be sufficient to enable the child to keep such behaviour private so that other children will not be disturbed by behaviour which they may not understand.

Dr Suzanne Sgroi (1988) suggests that childhood sexual behaviour and patterns of activity can be summarised in four stages. Stage 1, up to five years, is characterised by intense curiosity and includes masturbation and looking at others' bodies. Stage 2, during primary school years, typically includes game playing with peers and the previous curiosity is continued but in a more private, gamelike atmosphere. Stage 3, from ten to twelve years, or puberty is, of course, characterised by individuation and separation from parents and behaviours can then include sexual exposure and voyeurism. Stage 4, adolescence, is similar to adulthood and may include falling in love, sexual fondling and also simulated or actual intercourse.

During the process of assessment, then, we need to consider whether the sexualised behaviour is developmentally appropriate. If it is not, or if the behaviour is also persistent, aggressive, threatening or secretive, or if the victimised child is traumatised by the experience, then the event can be seen as abusive and appropriate action should be taken, even if the abusing child is in denial.

If, on early assessment, it is felt that the abusive behaviour is an attempt to resolve the trauma of witnessing or being the victim of sexual exploitation, then a short period of facilitative therapy may be sufficient to determine this. Of course, if this should prove to be the case, then all the necessary steps to protect the abusing child (as well as his or her victims) should be followed. Once the child is in a safe place, with supportive carers, the sexualised behaviour may cease, or may do so once the child has been able to sort out the problem in therapy.

A THERAPEUTIC PROGRAMME FOR AN ABUSING CHILD

For some children, however, a few sessions to help the confused child to understand his own trauma is not sufficient. If we look at the coping mechanisms described in chapter 3 and at the assessment procedure described in chapter 2 we may realise that, just like the Red Queen in *Alice*, the child is behaving in very controlling ways in many aspects of his life, not simply in the behaviour for which he has been referred.

One such child was George. At eight years old his behaviour in school was almost unmanageable. He was very intelligent and often managed to conceal his aggressive acts towards other children. He was sophisticated in his use of bribes and threats and he extricated pocket money and sweets from his classmates without detection by teachers. His diligent and concerned foster mother noticed his acquisition of goods which were not his and, eventually, his 'extortion racket' was uncovered, although George still denied his involvement, even in the face of clear evidence. When he was reminded that several children had witnessed him aggressively fondling a younger girl, he said that these other children were the real abusers and he had not been involved. Only after he was suspended from school did younger boys and girls begin to talk more freely about his abusive behaviour.

It was known that George had been physically and sexually abused by a very controlling stepfather for most of his life until he had been removed from home at the age of six. He felt he had been unable to protect his younger sister who was also abused. He also witnessed the physical and sexual abuse of his mother. He escaped from this environment, in which he was totally powerless, only when he was at nursery school and, later, at school. His defence, therefore, was to control as much as possible while he was out of the home. In his denial, rationalisation and projecting of his behaviour onto others, he was merely following the role model set by his stepfather.

It is clear that a child such as George not only needs therapy to help him to understand and to integrate his many abusive experiences, but he also needs help in controlling his anti-social and dangerous behaviour. For at least half of his young life he had been behaving in this controlling way, exploiting and abusing children younger or less powerful than himself. In some ways therefore he was not much different from a thirty-year-old sexual abuser who had been abusing others since adolescence. Both will need help in controlling their addictive behaviour and both will need support and suggestions for problem-solving in nonsexual and non-aggressive ways.

There is a difference, however, between the eight-year-old and the adult. The sexual and physical abuse of George stopped less than two years ago. A severe physical attack by his stepfather caused questions to be asked at school. George has still not been able to process any of this and has not been able to contain it either.

The abusing adult, on the other hand, may have been able to contain his own abusive childhood experiences sufficiently so that they do not now intrude into his daily living. As we saw, in the sexual abuse cycle, the offender is not actively remembering his own trauma but is, nevertheless, responding to it because he has negative expectations of events and he copes by exercising control over others. In doing this however, the adult has evolved a system of coping which is dangerous and addictive and the most urgent treatment work for him must be on his own addictive and abusive behaviour.

A child such as George, therefore, needs facilitating therapy more urgently than the abusing adult and this leads me to believe that this should always be carried out alongside a programme of behavioural modification. This hypothesis was confirmed by the research which I carried out with Eileen Gallagher (1995 & 1997). This was a small qualitative research project on six children who had been referred to the NSPCC (National Society for the Prevention of Cruelty to Children) in the North of England because they were sexually abusing other children. For the purposes of the research we concentrated on children who were aged twelve or under and, in fact, three of the children were eleven and three were twelve. This reflects the great reluctance amongst social workers, parents and children themselves to accept sexually abusive behaviour in younger children. We were well aware that children as young as seven were being referred to NSPCC teams but workers and parents, understandably, could not accept that this behaviour was exploitative. It is interesting to note that five out of the six children had several previously recorded instances of sexually aggressive behaviour and one had twenty-two instances. All these had been recorded from the age of seven or eight but no referrals, or further action, had been taken.

This was particularly worrying because all the children in the study had been involved in bullying at school, either as victims, perpetrators, or both. Recently, bullying in schools has been taken much more seriously and it is recognised that such behaviour is indicative of problems within the child which may need attention.

Five of the children in this study reported that they had been sexually abused. All six children had suffered trauma, including emotional abuse. Most of the social workers and therapists recognised that work had to be done on the child's own trauma and some also initiated cognitive behavioural and educative work on the offences themselves. According to Debelle et al. (1993) there is, as yet, little research to show that one treatment approach, or component, or combination, is better than another. Our small sample could not show this either, but, based on the reports of the children themselves, their carers and their social workers, it would seem that a combination of behavioural/educative techniques, and an empathic therapeutic response, is most effective. Effective work with the child's parents or carers was shown to be equally important, and this will be discussed further in chapter 8.

Psychodrama and dramatherapy can be used, of course, to rehearse or reinforce behaviours, and so can be part of the behavioural and educative component of a treatment programme for an abusing child as well as part of the empathic therapeutic component.

Eleven-year-old Holly was unable to be assertive without also getting angry. There were explosive and sometimes tearful outbursts at school when she found difficulty with her work or when her work was criticised. She had been sexually abused by a neighbour when she was nine. In one-to-one therapeutic sessions it had been ascertained that when she felt angry she would push younger children to the ground and expose their genitals. Assertiveness training was therefore important for her at this stage in her treatment. Firstly, in one-to-one sessions, she practised assertiveness by imagining that she was holding a precious object whilst the therapist walked slowly towards her. Holly also imagined that she had drawn a boundary line in front of her which the therapist must not cross. She practised shouting 'Stop' in a firm, non-aggressive way, until she felt confident. Then the therapist tried to give reasons why

Holly should relinquish the precious object and Holly practised giv-
ing her answers in a calm way. Eventually she progressed into a
group for young offenders where she was able to practise very
familiar situations, which happened at home or school, to which
she could respond in an assertive non-aggressive way. This was
part of a programme, together with family work, with her rather
controlling father and passive mother, and soon Holly's bullying
and sexual aggression stopped.

Of course, it is important that the use of psychodrama for role-
training should not precede a careful assessment and an exploration of the feelings of an abused and/or abusing child. Repeating
situations which cause the child to be angry, without any understanding of the roots of the anger, could reinforce the feeling of
helplessness which is the beginning of the abuse cycle for many
abusing children.

Similarly, the encouragement of expressions of anger in
psychodrama sessions with children who are abusing should be
treated with care. Often the abuse is a way of converting extremely angry feelings to action which feels less threatening and
over which the child feels in control. In psychodrama sessions,
therefore, the anger can be expressed in different ways from the
sexual abuse, but if the child chooses extremely violent actions
then this should be managed by the therapist who ensures that
the child, the therapist and the equipment in the room are not
damaged. If the violent expression persists, or if it threatens to
become uncontrolled, then the therapist should stop it and make
more creative suggestions about expressing it. Throwing clay at a
gloss-painted or tiled wall might suffice, or sloshing paint onto
large sheets of paper may be helpful. What must not happen is
that the child rehearses violent, abusive behaviour. This is
already happening in life and this must not be reinforced.

Harry was twelve and had been bullying other children at school
for some years. His father had abandoned him at an early age and
his mother, who had several younger children, had been unable to
control his aggressive behaviour. He had been in foster homes since
the age of six. During the therapeutic work with Harry he had
disclosed some early, fragmented memories of sexual abuse by his
father. Apparently his father used to force Harry to suck his penis.
This abuse may have started when Harry was a tiny baby and
must have stopped when his father left home when Harry was less
than two years old. Harry's bullying technique was to coerce a

friend into joining him in isolating a younger child, usually a girl, in a quiet part of the school or in grounds near the school. He would then ask the friend to hold the child whilst he forced his penis into her mouth. The 'friend' was usually coerced because of threats to tell about previous misdemeanours.

In group sessions with other abusing boys of a similar age he replayed a typical scene, reversing roles with his victim, so that he could experience those feelings. Of course the actual abuse was not re-enacted, the group leader asking Harry to stop the action at the crucial moment. The group then shared with Harry their own feelings of vulnerability and of power and he was able to talk of his own fears. He said that he felt he was going 'crazy' when he had flashbacks about his own abuse. He said he thought that he must be 'queer' when he remembered his father's penis. When he was able to express his fear and pain he was able to empathise with his own victim feelings, as well as those of the children he had victimised.

The importance of helping a child to change her distorted cognition of herself and of previous events is illustrated in the following description. This is an extreme example of a child who appears to have been abused in bizarre and ritualised ways by several abusers, including her mother.

Irene was twelve years old and had some learning difficulties. She could read and write, however, and could draw well. Drawing was her preferred method of working during the therapeutic sessions and she would often add words to her drawings, in the manner of a comic strip, which was her favourite reading material. She had often drawn 'the devil', a red-faced figure with horns, and she had drawn strange 'charts' with odd shapes on them. On this occasion she drew a house containing two dead children. One was lying on the floor with a bleeding wound in her chest and the other was hanging from a beam. She drew herself wearing a crown which was topped with candles and said she was 'only three years old' but she was 'a King'. In her right hand she carried a knife which was dripping with blood. She also included her mother, who was smiling as she watched the scene from behind a barred window, and 'the devil' who was also smiling through a barred window. The dead children had sad faces, in contrast to the others in the picture.

In a very matter-of-fact voice Irene explained that she was a 'bad' person, and so was her mother, but that her mother could be excused because she was ruled by 'the devil'. The therapist asked if Irene could also be excused similarly but Irene said she had chosen to kill the two children. She then added quietly that if she had not killed the children she herself would have been killed. The therapist wondered what it would be like to have such a terrible choice. Irene replied that she had no choice.

This drawing, of course, bizarre and frightening as it was, could have started an investigation into abusive and ritualised practices in Irene's extended family. However, investigations into the sexual abuse of Irene by both parents had been concluded when she was five years old. The parents had disappeared and Irene had been put into foster care. She had progressed well but had just been referred for therapy because she had been sexually fondling a younger child. Again she had responded well to firm behavioural guidance from her foster mother and the therapist. In addition, the social workers had made sure that clear safety factors were instituted both in Irene's school and in the foster home, with regard to other, younger children and the abusive behaviour seemed to be controlled.

However, the onset of puberty was perhaps reviving some disturbing memories for Irene and from the drawing the therapist was able to map her perception of herself as follows:

IRENE'S PERCEPTION

I AM BAD
(I KILL PEOPLE)

I CHOSE TO BE BAD
(UNLIKE MY MOTHER WHO HAD NO CHOICE)

I WOULD RATHER BE BAD THAN DEAD
(COPING STRATEGY)

In questioning what it would be like to make such a choice the therapist was asking Irene to empathise with her three-year-old self, which she had previously been unable to do. As she replied 'I had no choice' Irene was at last showing some victim empathy (with herself at three). The therapist was helping Irene to change her perception of herself from 'a bad person who was in control' to a victim who did not have a choice then but, because she was now a survivor, did have a choice now. The important therapeutic points here are that the therapist did not deny Irene's perception of herself by saying 'You are not bad, you were a child who had no choice', but accepted the perception, merely asking what it must have felt like to be in that position. In this way Irene was able to question her own cognition and to begin the journey of changing this.

Irene's sexually abusing behaviour (fondling a younger child) was typical for a child perpetrator. Toni Cavanagh Johnson (1988) who has done a great deal of research in this area, found that 'fondling' (with hands) was easily the most typical behaviour of children who abuse, followed by direct genital contact without penetration and then, perhaps surprising, by penetration of anus with penis. Some paediatricians in Britain have been stating for some time that they are worried by the signs of anal penetration which they discover in many children whom they are asked to examine. It may be, therefore, that those children who abuse others by penetrating them anally are repeating their own abuse, or it may be possible that some of the abused children who are being examined are being abused by other children. Cavanagh Johnson also discovered in her research that 72% of the youngest abusing children had definitely been sexually abused, although this figure fell to 42% in seven- to ten-year-olds and 35% in eleven- to twelve-year-olds. Of course these figures show only children where abuse had been proved and not those where abuse might be suspected.

One feature of sexual abuse by adults is the amount of coercion used on the children. In any treatment programme for perpetrators this feature is always raised and discussed even though abusers often deny coercion. Many children are afraid of adult offenders and believe they will be harmed, or members of their family will be harmed, if they do not comply. Some children are told by a parental abuser that he will go to prison if she tells and then she will have no one to care for her. Others are threatened with bizarre punishments which a child cannot evaluate and realise that they would be impossible to carry out. Many children, for instance, are told that their parents will be told that the child has initiated the abuse and therefore that the parents will punish the child rather than the adult. Others are told that their parents will be told of other misdemeanours which the child has committed such as smoking or drinking (cigarettes or alcohol having been supplied by the abuser).

Child abusers also coerce their victims into compliance as Cavanagh Johnson also found in her research, 60% using verbal coercion and 17% using physical coercion. Gail Ryan states that many children bribe others to comply with money, treats, favours or friendship. To a child who is already victimised, or bullied, friendship can be a powerful coercive tool. Older children, including older siblings, often use their age or role in the family as a powerful coercive factor. They also use trickery, knowing that a younger child is easily tricked and manipulated into 'secret' behaviour which may seem desirable because the older child is admired or emulated.

Helping a child to understand how he has misused his power to coerce a victim is one example of the changes in cognition which need to be worked on with an abusing child. Another example is in the use of the sexual abuse cycle which, we have already explained, is used with adults and with adolescents. With children, however, it may be simpler to use the idea of 'Steps to Getting Into Trouble' instead of the 'Abuse Cycle'. Kee MacFarlane (1991) shows the way in which she adapts this for young children. She uses 'Steps' to show the progression from 'Feeling Bad' to the actual 'Sexual Abuse'. I have written these progressive feelings below eight 'steps', (see Figure 6.2), and I have written the comments of an eleven-year-old abuser with whom I have worked, above each step. In therapy the child personalises the feelings by adding his own statements and explanations of how he feels during the time immediately before an abusive act.

COMPONENTS OF A DUAL PROGRAMME FOR YOUNG SEXUAL ABUSERS

As we have seen, a programme for children who are sexually abusing should contain the dual components of treatment of the perpetration behaviour and of the child's own victimisation. These can be sorted into the following elements:

PERPETRATION	VICTIMISATION
Managing anger	Addressing victim trauma
Teaching problem-solving skills	Building self-esteem
Education on sexuality	Countering sex role stereotyping
Building victim empathy	Assertiveness training

My experience has shown that it is usually unproductive for a therapist to try to give input to both perpetration and victimisation parts of the programme. The person who works with the child on perpetration needs to be more confronting, more chal-

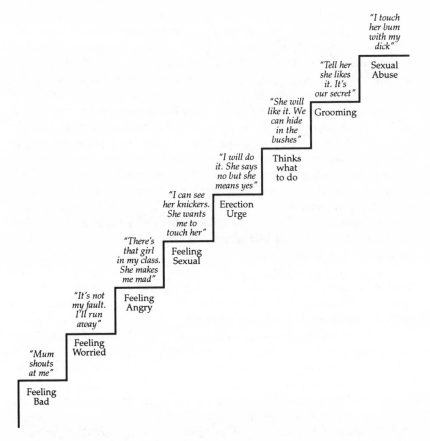

Figure 6.2 Steps to getting into trouble

lenging, than the person who works on the victimisation issues. In addition it is sometimes the case that a child is referred for therapy before both sides of the story are known. That is, a child may be referred because of his own abuse and it is only in therapy that his abuse of others is revealed. Alternatively, a child may be referred because of abusive acts and only then is his own abuse revealed.

The two therapists need to be in communication and the young person needs to know this but confidentiality must be respected, within the agreed limits, if this is part of the contract made with the young person. Of course, if a second therapist is introduced at a later stage the agreement or contract with the child will have to be changed to meet the prevailing circumstances.

In addition there is a further duality in a programme for young offenders. It is vital for there to be simultaneous work with the parents or carers of the young perpetrator. The parents will need to understand the situations which can trigger anger, which may be the forerunners of perpetration behaviour. The parents' own problem-solving skills may be limited and they too can benefit from similar help, which will assist them with helping their children. It may well be also that these parents will need some education on sexuality and sex role stereotyping. It is likely that some parents of abusing children will have encouraged their child to blame the victim. An understanding of coercion and the lack of choice for young victims is, therefore, also important for the parents or carers to have. Low self-esteem may also be a feature with one or both parents and this may be exacerbated by the knowledge that they are now parents of an offending child. Some help in this area is, therefore, usually necessary.

The whole question of parallel work with the parents of children who have been abused will be addressed in chapter 8 but it should be remembered that for children who are also abusers, this work is more specific. It is often very helpful to such parents if they can meet in a group which runs at the same time as a treatment group for their children. Both groups have their own confidentiality, of course, but there is consultation between the facilitators of the groups, who may have joint planning or debriefing sessions or, perhaps, a joint supervisor. In this way specific confidentiality is maintained but both groups can have some understanding of what the other group is doing so that fantasies are allayed. If this is not done, both parents and children can sabotage the work which is being done in the parallel group because they fear that personal or family secrets are being exposed.

We have seen that work with young sexual abusers is complicated and requires heavy resources. In terms of prevention, however, the rewards are high. We know from the literature that many abusers have committed hundreds of offences before they are caught. They hardly ever stop, as a result of being caught, unless they receive prolonged treatment. In a lifetime of offending, therefore, an abuser could easily abuse 7,000 to 8,000 times. This could be with as few as fifty children or the offences could be directed against thousands of children. It will be seen that work with young people, before they embark on a career of offending, is vitally important.

7 WORKING WITH DIFFERENCE

Bernadette danced with Matt ... other girls seemed too scared of him ... Such treatment is one of the griefs of the blind, and Matt could tell when it happened ...

from *Homebush Boy*,
by Thomas Keneally

The concept of difference is a difficult one for many of us to accept. In order to understand our fellow human beings we often look for similarities to ourselves and ignore differences. If the differences are too apparent for us to ignore then we tend to categorise people and to make generalisations. On the issue of gender, for instance, there are many studies which show that we treat male and female babies very differently. In tests where baby boys and baby girls were dressed to suggest that they were the opposite gender, adults watching them on videotape attributed characteristics such as bravery to the children dressed as boys and more passive attributes to the children dressed as girls.

Even after the Second World War when the Holocaust was recognised and fascism exposed, there was a great deal of racial discrimination in the Western world. Assumptions were still made about people, based on the colour of their skin alone. In an effort to combat this a movement arose in which similarities were stressed and differences were ignored. In Britain black children were often fostered or adopted by white families who had no experience of caring for children of other cultures. Often a black child was the only one in a white neighbourhood.

People with disabilities have also been discriminated against, even to the point of being hidden out of sight, or of being feared. Debate still rages on whether children with learning difficulties should be separately educated or integrated into classrooms with other more able children.

Differences in sexuality are very confusing for most children. Many cultures discriminate against homosexuality and often laws are different for young people who are heterosexual and those who are not. The age of consent, for instance, is sixteen for heterosexuals and eighteen for homosexual males in Britain. Popular culture also stigmatises young, gay men who feel their 'difference' keenly. Attitudes to lesbians also vary widely according to class and environment.

Children who have been sexually abused often feel very different from other children. When we looked at the models for understanding abuse we were reminded by Finkelhor & Browne (1985) that 'Stigma' is one of the dynamics which cause trauma and distress. Girls, for instance, can be labelled as 'damaged goods' in cultures where females are still seen as property. Abused girls often feel that they must have invited the abuse and that this is because they are inherently 'bad'. Boys who have been abused by men feel that they are labelled as homosexual and fear that something in their demeanour caused the offences against them. Helping an adolescent boy to feel comfortable with his sexuality, whether heterosexual or homosexual, then becomes more difficult.

CHILDREN FIRST?

Those of us who have worked with children for many years have often had a policy of 'Children First', which indicates that children are not inferior adults but have particular needs because of their stage of development. This approach can be helpful but not if it is carried out to the point where differences in children are not acknowledged. Margaret Kennedy (1996: 129–30), a well-known writer on children with disability, states 'it is potentially ... damaging to insist that disabled children are children first and foremost and that methods of working with non-disabled children are just as appropriate. Taking the "children first" position means that the reality of impairment – and the needs associated with it – can be denied.'

This statement also holds good for other areas of difference. The task of the therapist is to acknowledge that each child is unique. In making an agreement with an abused child, at the commencement of therapy, it is essential to acknowledge that abuse has occurred. It may well be that identity issues for a black child or a disabled child become very apparent as the work commences. It may even transpire that the vulnerability of such a child has been highlighted by the abuse and that it is the issue of race or disability which needs to be tackled first and foremost. An autistic child, or one with severe learning difficulties, may present immediate communication problems but we cannot assume that this disability is the primary factor in the child's presentation.

Jasmine was a tall, fourteen-year-old girl who came to see the therapist with her parents, a black couple who had come to Britain from Jamaica. Jasmine had been diagnosed as having severe learning difficulties with some autistic tendencies. She appeared to have about a dozen words of vocabulary but she communicated fairly well with her mother through gestures, looks and a few words. She had been sexually abused whilst having a week's 'respite care', which had been organised to enable her mother to have a break and to give more time to her other three children.

Jasmine moved around the therapy room several times, touching items delicately and repetitively as if to confirm that they really existed. She did not protest when her parents left the room and she settled down in a corner with a collection of rag dolls. The therapist sat down beside her and commented on the dolls. Some of them were adult and some were child dolls and in addition they represented black, Asian and white cultures. Jasmine showed no sign that she had heard anything which the therapist had said but she picked out an adult, male, white doll and threw it towards the window. Then she picked up a female, child, black doll and rocked it gently. The therapist continued her commentary, remarking that 'the man' had gone now and that Jasmine was caring for 'the little girl'. After a while she stood up and pulled the therapist to her feet. She said 'toilet' so the therapist accompanied her to the bathroom, which was across the corridor. Jasmine was still carrying the black doll. The therapist had already ascertained with Jasmine's mother, Rose, that Jasmine could toilet herself perfectly well so after she had shown her the facilities, she prepared to withdraw. Jasmine grabbed her arm and mimed that she should stay, then she went to the taps and turned them on full so that they made a great noise. 'Whoosh, whoosh' said Jasmine, becoming increasingly agitated. She moved towards the toilet compartment and mimed the taking down of her underclothes. Then she placed the black doll on the closed seat of the toilet. 'Jack', she said, looking frightened. Then in an extraordinarily powerful and painful action Jasmine mimed someone entering the compartment, grabbing the black doll and sexually molesting her. She rocked the doll again and left the bathroom abruptly.

The therapist was able to ascertain from Rose that it was this mime which she had already enacted for her mother which alerted her to the fact of her child's abuse. Staff at the care centre found it difficult to accept that one of their number had been abusing a child and, since few of the children in the centre had speech, it was not easy to obtain corroboration. It was ascertained, however, that it was entirely possible that 'Jack' had abused Jasmine in the bathroom and had used the noise of the taps to disguise any sound of protest from the child. Rose never used the care facility again but she persisted in her diligent inquiries. Eventually it was discovered that 'Jack' had a history of suspected offences against children in other settings.

After working with Jasmine for some time, and also working separately with her mother, the (white) therapist felt confident that Jasmine was secure in her black identity as a much-loved member of her family in an immigrant part of the city where she lived. In addition, Rose had gone to considerable trouble to read the literature on children with similar disabilities and was giving her every opportunity to fulfil her potential, without having unrealistic expectations. Jasmine also appeared to be accepted well by her siblings and in the day-care facility which she attended for a few hours each week.

In parallel sessions with Rose, however, it became apparent that she was not coping at all well with her daughter's sexual abuse and she felt she must immediately stop Jasmine if she tried to communicate with her mother anything about the incidents. The therapist suspected that Rose had been sexually abused herself and Rose confirmed this in a tearful session. This was the first time she had disclosed the abuse which had occurred in Jamaica when she was ten years old. The painful feelings, which had been stimulated by Jasmine's disclosure, were almost too much to bear so she had found herself unable to listen to her child. It was therefore not surprising that Jasmine, who had been used to a mother who had creatively 'listened' to her, found it difficult to understand why her mother was now reluctant to help her.

Of course the issue of disability was a complicating factor. Rose, like many other people, found it difficult to accept that a disabled child might have a sexual life and so the issues of Jasmine's sexuality had never been addressed. Again, like most people, she had also assumed that no one would abuse a child with disabilities. Rose's strictly religious upbringing also inhibited her from talking about sexuality. The therapist, therefore, worked slowly and carefully with Jasmine, mostly using the large rag dolls, to act as a witness to the confusing and frightening events which had happened.

She then discovered that Jasmine liked to draw and through this medium they worked together on issues of fear and vulnerability and also on matters of sex education. Eventually Rose felt able to join the sessions herself and to continue the dialogue with her daughter. In her own therapy sessions Rose addressed the fact that Jasmine had been showing some fear of white males since the abuse. Because of this Jasmine's father had been making some racist remarks about white men. Rose was able to tell him about her own abuse, by a black man, and her husband became more supportive, both of Rose and of Jasmine. Eventually Rose joined a women's group working against the oppression of women and of black women in particular.

SEXUAL ABUSE IN DIFFERENT CULTURES

The issue of race and sexual abuse can also become entangled in a different way, as illustrated by Khadj Rouf (1990: 17–18). She was abused by her father, a Bangladeshi. Rouf's mother, a white woman, and her female cousin, from Bangladesh, both supported her when she finally disclosed that she had been sexually abused for over eight years. After group therapy she stated that she was able to accept her identity and to call herself proudly 'mixed race', whereas before she could not accept the Asian part of herself because it represented her father. Asian girls and young women have also said that they could not disclose their abuse to white teachers or social workers because of the feeling that they would be 'letting down their race or their Muslim culture'.

As we saw with Sharnaz, in an earlier chapter, it may be helpful to use dolls of different ethnicity to encourage Asian and black children to re-enact feelings and it is also necessary for the therapist to be aware of differing religious and cultural expectations. Of course dolls of different ethnic groups should be available for all children, both black and white. In creating a child-friendly room it is also important that the pictures and decorations in the room reflect a multi-cultural perspective and also a perspective which includes children with disability. A therapist cannot, however, be well informed on all the differences in children's expectations which appear in today's society. Sometimes it is necessary to take specialist advice.

Kariba arrived in Britain from an African country with her father and younger brother. They were on a visit to Kariba's aunt, her father's sister, who had lived in Britain for many years. Kariba's father was offered a job by a relative, and so he stayed on, illegally, with the children, then aged eleven and thirteen. They attended local schools and Kariba and her brother wrote regularly to their mother, who had stayed in Africa with two more younger children. Their mother also ran a business and so she was kept busy, although she often included a note for the children in her letters to her husband.

Kariba's father had always physically chastised his children in a severe manner but when he began to abuse her sexually she tried to tell her aunt, who refused to believe her. Kariba then wrote to her mother but had to do this clandestinely because usually her notes were read by her father and enclosed by him in his own letters home. Eventually her mother managed to travel to Britain with her younger children and Kariba's father, when confronted with medical evidence, admitted the offence and escaped back to Africa.

There then followed a protracted battle for Kariba's mother and the children to remain in Britain and at this point an adviser who specialised in the customs of Kariba's country was called in to enable the officials to realise the danger in which Kariba and her mother stood if she was deported. Kariba's school performance and her behaviour deteriorated and she was also referred for therapy.

The therapist tried to discuss Kariba's situation with her but felt continually that Kariba was 'blocked' or 'frozen'. Kariba said she was happy to 'do some acting' and soon she was trying to enact small scenes showing her current feelings. The overwhelming feeling was of extreme fear and, in fact, Kariba was sure that her father, or one of his friends, would kill her. The therapist felt that this was unlikely and tried to desensitise Kariba by rehearsing imagined future scenes as well as past scenes when Kariba felt able. She also did some assertiveness exercises with Kariba and tried to reassure her that the threat of deportation was now removed. The therapist was still puzzled at Kariba's poor response however, until she contacted the adviser who had been helpful in explaining the position to the Home Office. The adviser was able to convince the therapist that the patriarchal power and the lack of law and order in this particular small African country was such that Kariba's fears may be well-founded. From this point, with the therapist and Kariba working together on the issue of fear, Kariba began to improve.

This example once again illustrates the necessity for moving at the child's pace. The therapist had noted that Kariba and her mother were both of above average intelligence. She knew that her mother had been running her own business and had dealt with officialdom and bureaucracy in the UK in order to protect her children and herself. Neither was Kariba's mother worn down by abuse of herself, although all the children had certainly been severely chastised in an abusive fashion. It was, however, very difficult for her and Kariba to accept that there could be any protection for them if her husband chose to retaliate either in person or through 'a friend'. It was only possible to move forward with Kariba when a network of helpers from a domestic violence agency, a local church and a community centre, was in place.

Kariba and her family were recent immigrants but black families who have lived in Britain for some time will be very aware of the discrimination which is faced constantly. Rhonda Siddall (1994) quotes a thirty-year-old black woman who had been sexually abused by members of her extended family. 'You see, as a black girl, I had experienced a lot of negative things anyway, so you learn not to question too much.' This learned powerlessness can, of course, also apply to other groups, such as children who are disabled.

Many studies in the US include black and Hispanic children, in populations where these groups are represented, and most show that the incidence of abuse in these groups is similar to the ethnicity of the population in those areas. Few studies, however, specifically target black children and look at how abuse may affect them differently from white children. Lois Pierce and Robert L. Pierce (1984) did an excellent study of 56 black children, compared with 149 white children, who had been sexually abused. The main differences in the characteristics of the families was that fewer black children had a natural father living at home and the white children were more likely to be abused by their natural fathers. The black children were more likely to be abused by stepfathers or 'uncles' (who, Pierce states, may have been mother's friends).

This might be expected but more striking are the comments of the abused black children about their feelings regarding the abuse. Few of these children were afraid that their family would break up or that they would not be believed if they told, although both these factors were important for white children and often contributed to delay in telling. The children's feelings were confirmed by the mothers. Very few black mothers rejected their child's disclosure of abuse, whereas nearly a quarter of the white mothers did. A few of the white mothers also encouraged the abuse and stated that they feared violence from the perpetrator. None of the black mothers encouraged the abuse although a small percentage also feared violence from the perpetrator.

Regarding the implications for treatment, Pierce and Pierce suggest that family therapy is inappropriate for black families. Of course, when this study was published, in 1984, family therapy was probably the most popular treatment, based on Henry and Anna Giaretto's work in California. Since then, however, as we have seen, the appropriateness of this type of therapy in all families where sexual abuse has occurred has been questioned. However, there may be a misunderstanding that family therapy must necessarily include all members, including the abuser. It is my experience that after individual work and/or group work has been carried out with the abused children and, separately, with their parents, then some joint work, firstly in pairs, and then as a group, will often be necessary before family members can continue to support each other.

Pierce and Pierce also make the point that the issue of power is particularly important for black families, for whom powerlessness in society is a norm and so the understanding of powerlessness in abuse, which I have discussed in earlier chapters, is very pertinent. They also quote studies which show that black women may have differing views of their own sexuality and that this should, therefore, be taken into account when working with black children. This bears out the differences we found with Kariba's mother, whose strong religious beliefs affected her understanding of her own sexuality.

During many years of training child protection workers in Ireland I have also found that strong religious beliefs, which may include views on the sanctity of marriage, may affect the rates of disclosure of abuse. It may also affect the vulnerability of some children who are not given sufficient sexual knowledge to protect themselves. During therapy, therefore, some of these children will need education about sexual matters but this can only be done with full co-operation from the non-abusing parent.

One of the key differences which Pierce and Pierce found, but did not discuss, was that black mothers (who were often single parents) were generally more supportive of their abused children. As we will discuss in the next chapter, this kind of support is essential if children are to receive maximum benefit from the therapy.

ABUSE OF DISABLED CHILDREN

Westcott and Cross (1996) have pointed out the reluctance of many therapists to work with disabled children. There are still problems with inaccessible buildings and fears from therapists that they will not be able to understand children who communicate through boards such as Makaton. Many therapists (including myself) have worked more frequently with learning disabled, rather than physically disabled, children. I have always felt that the therapeutic goals for abused children with learning difficulties should be similar to those for other abused children. Indeed Sullivan and Scanlan (1987: 153–6) who specialise in work with sexually abused children who have learning disabilities, list treatment goals which are universal for children who have been sexually abused. These are:

- To alleviate guilt engendered by the sexual abuse and to assist the child in regaining the ability to trust peers and adults.

- To help treat the depression that is often manifested by children who have been sexually abused.

- To help the child learn to express anger relating to the sexual abuse in appropriate and productive ways.

- To teach basic information about normal human sexuality and interpersonal relationships.

- To teach the child sexual preference and homosexual issues, when appropriate.

- To teach sexual issues, when appropriate.

- To teach the child self-protection techniques.

- The development of an affective vocabulary to label emotions and feelings.

- The attainment of emotional independence.

- Assistance in the establishment of a meaningful and stable identity.

- Development of a personal value system.

- The development of a capacity for lasting relationships and for both tender and genital love.

- Treatment of secondary behavioural characteristics.

However, accomplishing these goals depends on providing a therapeutic programme in which each child is enabled to succeed. Because each child is unique, therapy must be eclectic and tailored to the individual.

As we saw with Beattie and with Alison in the opening chapter, communication with an abused child who also has learning and speech difficulties is possible if empathy is established and the therapist enables the child to have some control. My own hearing problems have enabled me to develop a technique where I repeat a child's words to ensure that I have heard correctly. The psychodramatic technique of doubling also enables me to verbalise feelings which a child cannot express. This technique should be used with caution, however, in a child with speech difficulties who expects others to 'speak for her'. She may become angry if she feels the therapist is doing this or she may passively agree with the 'doubling' because she is tired of correcting workers who assume her needs.

After explaining the technique it is always advisable to ask an abused child whether she will allow doubling. It is important that the child at least nods if the doubling is correct or shakes her head if it is not. Of course a child who cannot do this may communicate through a Bliss/Makaton/Rebus board. A therapist who is not familiar with this equipment may choose to work with someone who is. Therapists for abused children must always be prepared to work alongside or take advice from others. Once a rapport with a child has been established it is no more difficult to double for a disabled child than for one who is more able. If another worker is present in the sessions then care must be taken to ensure that their role is clear, both to them, and to the child. Of course, having any intermediary, such as an interpreter for a child who does not have English as a first language, may present problems with confidentiality. I have found that in a group for abused adolescent girls, for instance, the best interpreters are the other children in the group. They will have the necessary understanding of the situation and of the feelings engendered.

As Sullivan and Scanlan point out in their list, the development of a meaningful identity may have particular emphasis for a disabled child.

Len was nine years old and had learning difficulties and 'behavioural problems'. He had been sexually abused by a family friend who had offered to take care of him for weekends to relieve his professional parents who had two other, more able, older children. Len had a habit of 'gurning' (pulling faces) and often this was unconscious and compulsive. However, sometimes he stood in front of the mirror in the therapy room and stared at himself whilst gurning in a particularly alarming fashion. 'What is that face saying?' asked the therapist. Len did not reply but picked up a pad of 'stickers' lying on the table. 'Spell STUPID' he commanded. The therapist spelled it out. He wrote the word and stuck the label on his forehead, returning to the mirror grimacing violently.

Work with Len had to start in the place where he was. He believed that he was stupid and worthless and the sexual abuse was merely another humiliation in his life. It was extremely difficult to help Len to believe that he had a meaningful identity because his family, although sincere in their wish for Len to 'get better', could not recognise his qualities. When he was temporarily removed from his family for a few weeks the gurning almost stopped and he was more able to express other issues with the therapist. Eventually Len was removed permanently to another family who were more able to see and love his essential self.

In Britain Valerie Sinason is noted for her work with learning disabled children at the Tavistock Clinic. In a paper (Sinason 1988), she describes how, during child observation sessions, she saw a child being bathed by his mother. All the mother's movements were gentle and loving except that when she wiped the baby's mouth the movement was brisk and the child reacted by screwing up his eyes and pulling up his legs. This procedure was repeated over six months but as the weeks progressed the child accepted the rough treatment of the mouth and began to smile and stare at the mother as soon as she touched his mouth. The mother then remarked how much the child liked the rough movement. Sinason describes this as a tiny piece of everyday abuse in an above average home and goes on to show how she believes such a child is corrupted into believing that abusive acts are not so.

In a day nursery for physically abused children I have also often seen parents (often fathers) handling their small children very roughly, sometimes picking them up with one arm and swinging them. If a nursery nurse intervened, the parent would then state that the child (who was sometimes screaming) really enjoyed the movement. The child would often be smiling and the screams were attributed to squeals of delight, although occasionally there were spontaneous tears as well. These children had suffered broken limbs, severe bruising, fractured skulls and so on but they had accommodated to their treatment and bonded with the abusing parent or parents.

Sinason calls this process 'smiling, swallowing, sickening and stupefying' and she uses it to show how a child who is sexually abused within the family, over a period of time, can also smile, swallow the pain and eventually may sicken and become 'stupid'. She believes that children accommodate the abusing parental adult for their own survival and that some children can become 'mentally handicapped' through this process. She gives several examples to illustrate her point.

Roland Summit (1983) calls this process the Child Sexual Abuse Accommodation Syndrome. His research shows that children do accommodate the sexual abuse to ensure their survival, as Sinason claims, and that this can lead to guilt, low self-esteem and, of course, denial that their experiences were abusive. Alice Miller (1987b) cites numerous examples of adults who have accommodated their own physical abuse. She quotes a Czech author who spoke admiringly of his talented father who regularly beat his son. He stated that the beatings did him no harm, that they prepared him for life and made him hard and able to 'grit his teeth'. Sometimes this 'normalisation' of abuse leads to the abused child becoming abusive to others, as we have seen in the chapter on children who abuse.

Sinason is claiming that some degree of learning difficulty can be a result of sexual abuse and this is certainly my experience. Frequently children have been referred to me, having been 'statemented' by educational psychologists who have diagnosed 'mental handicap' (in the former use of the phrase) or 'learning difficulty' in the more acceptable modern form. The label 'stupid' is a difficult one to remove, especially if the child has placed it on himself through accommodation. Such a child will require a long period of therapy to overcome the abuse because of the underlying distortion of personality.

To touch or not to touch?

The issue of whether to touch an abused child becomes especially important when working with children with disabilities. The general rule is for the therapist to ask herself whether a proposed touching of a child is for the child's benefit or the therapist's. If it is to reassure the therapist then the touch is probably not helpful. On the other hand some children who have been sexually abused have said that they felt that they were not touched by workers because they were 'dirty'. Nonsexual touching can sometimes be helpful and dramatherapists have devised ways of working with touch which can help some children to desensitise themselves to their fear of touching or being touched.

Jenny Pearson (1996) describes Movement with Touch and the work of Marian Lindkvist. This work was pioneered with people who were mentally disabled and was also used successfully with autistic children. Pearson describes Movement with Touch as communicating and responding in a physical way, picking up the feelings from the client's body language and responding with the body. The process involves touching, hand against hand, foot against foot, or sometimes back to back. This, of course, should only be done by someone trained in the method but it is not too different from doubling or mirroring a client in a psychodramatic or dramatherapeutic way. This process can, of course, be used with many children who have physical as well as severe mental disabilities.

Children with mild learning difficulties who are afraid of touch because they have been abused, can be helped with simple dramatherapeutic exercises.

In a group for sexually abused adolescent girls the therapist asked the children to choose a partner with whom they felt comfortable. The therapist then demonstrated, with one of the girls, how to 'mirror' the movements of the other person by facing them and copying their movements, as if in a mirror. The pairs enjoyed this exercise in which each person had a chance to lead. The therapist then suggested a 'back to back' exercise in which the children tried to rise from a sitting position by leaning against the partner. At each stage the therapist was careful to ensure that any child who felt uncomfortable need not take part. Eventually, after a series of exercises, over a period of an hour, the children were able to hold hands and move in a circle which included the therapist, and were also able to play a game of 'Blind Man's Buff'. This game is very threatening for some abused children, both in the covering of the eyes for the person who is 'it', and in enduring the touch which is necessary to identify the person caught. It must be stressed that this exercise should not be carried out in a new group but was done expressly to help girls who were concerned about their own difficulties in giving and receiving touch.

Jenny Pearson also stresses the use of stamping movements for those with autistic tendencies. This acts as a grounding and releases pent-up energy. I have found that repetitive movements, carried out to music or to a rhythmic clapping, can help such children to appear more in touch with the world. As we saw with Jasmine, earlier in this chapter, repetitive, compulsive moving around or touching of objects is common in children with autistic tendencies. Perhaps the acceptance and harnessing of this tendency is simply using the child's own healing potential.

Most children (and adults) with learning difficulties can use role play to learn social skills. Several mental health facilities in hospitals employ workers to run groups for this purpose. Children who have been abused may lack social skills, not necessarily because of their learning difficulties but because they may have been deliberately isolated by abusing carers or parents. Similarly, some children who have been removed from their homes because of abuse, and placed in institutions, may appear to have learning difficulties because of their self-belief that they are 'stupid' and they may lack social skills because they have not had the opportunity to learn them in some children's homes.

After a period of one-to-one assessment, such children may best be served in small dramatherapy groups. Working obliquely through the metaphor of stories is often the most productive way forward although some adolescent children also enjoy using factual accounts of incidents from newspapers. If reading is a problem the therapist can read several, brief accounts and the children can choose the one they wish to enact. Alternatively, news reports can be audio- or videotaped and played to the young people. This kind of work is akin to sociodrama, which Moreno also invented, in which social situations or dilemmas (e.g. the AIDS issue, abortion) are explored through taking roles and acting certain scenes.

As Jasmine's mother illustrated, it may be difficult for some people to believe that children with disabilities can also be abused. One of my earliest experiences was of realising that the blind sister of a sexually abused girl had been present in the room during each time the girl was abused by their father. Although not directly assaulted by the father, the sister was severely traumatised, not least by her inability to understand what was happening, and by the threats imposed by the abuser to ensure that she did not tell. Children with visual impairments are, of course, also abused directly and can often be worked with using sensory materials such as clay and also, sometimes, with music.

Merry had very low vision, being able to distinguish not much more than darkness and light. At ten years old she had an attractive singing voice and enjoyed singing and composing popular songs. She sang into a tape recorder to compose her songs and so this was incorporated into her therapy for the sexual abuse she had suffered for a year, from a voluntary helper. She said to the therapist, 'When I sing I go somewhere else, like out of my body where I can feel things.' It may be that she had desensitised her body to the abuse while it was happening. Now she was afraid to express feelings except through her music. She checked out that the therapist understood what was happening. 'When I sing about the rain and the sun I can feel them again.' Gradually, in sessions where Merry sang and talked as she felt able, she was restored to the loving and confident girl she had been before the abuse. She still carried on singing.

Sullivan (1993) states that 'handicapped children characteristically have difficulties generalizing concepts in a specific situation, such as a therapy setting, to appropriate settings outside therapy where these concepts are applicable'. She suggests therefore that when working with a child on self-protection skills, at the end of a therapeutic programme, the child should be taken to an actual classroom, gymnasium, van, etc. so that he or she can be clear about exhibiting the learned skills in particular situations.

I would suggest that the use of psychodrama can cut out the need for such field trips to specific locations. In psychodrama we can create a location within the therapy or playroom. Firstly the child determines the boundaries of the room or place she is creating. A disabled child may need some help from the therapist with this but as much physical movement as possible should be encouraged so that the child truly begins to recreate the setting. Then the therapist invites the child to describe the furniture or fitments in the place. Whatever senses the child has should be brought into play. For instance 'What did this smell like?' will be an appropriate question for most children, not simply one who cannot see. Asking children to remember feelings of warmth or cold and to remember textures of materials, such as wooden seats or tiled walls can also help to recreate the familiar feel of an environment.

Once the scene has been recreated psychodramatically then the role play which rehearses future behaviour can begin. It is at this later stage in therapy that a group for children may be most effective and often all the children can learn from the role play which has been devised for one particular child.

The psychodramatic technique of recreating a setting can, of course, be used somewhat earlier in the therapy when working on the actual abuse which occurred. However, recreating the abusive setting should be done with caution and with appropriate safeguards. With adults and with most adolescents the therapist can ask that the protagonist remembers a place where she felt absolutely safe, and recreates this in the therapy room. The protagonist can then return to this safe place at any point during a difficult session. Occasionally this can be effective with children too, usually if they have spontaneously created their own 'safe place' in the therapy room at an early stage. As we saw with Beattie, in chapter 1, a young child, especially one like Beattie, with communication difficulties, may hide in a safe place for many of the early sessions. It would be unlikely, though, that Beattie would feel safe enough to re-enact her abuse, at least until she was older and at a later stage in her therapy.

Some children can return to the scene of the abuse by using 'a double' to play themselves in the scene. In an adult psychodrama group this is often done, but for most children in a group it would be too threatening to ask a child, who had herself been abused, to role play the abuse of another child. It is possible, however, for the therapist to play this role if the child spontaneously chooses to play the abuser.

Neil, aged five, had speech problems. Consonants were missing from most of his speech and, although he was now receiving speech therapy, it was still very difficult to understand him. He had been physically and sexually abused by his uncle, who lived with the family. He enjoyed puppet play and he used the animal puppets to express his feelings. He always took on the aggressive role of the Tiger puppet and managed to make it clear to the therapist that her puppets (usually pigs or sheep) should react to him with fear and submission. The therapist complied for several sessions, until she felt confident that Neil was ready to look at change. The next time he attacked her puppet she protested loudly and gathered reinforcements from other puppets to confront the Tiger. After his initial surprise Neil rapidly dropped the Tiger puppet and picked up a small dog puppet. 'Friend' he said, quite clearly, lining it up with the victim pig puppet of the therapist. Neil's therapy, and his communication difficulties, improved and progressed well from that point.

POWER AND OPPRESSION

Children with difference may feel stigmatised and so may children who have been sexually abused, as Finkelhor suggested. It is therefore important that abused children are not simply told that it is not their fault. They need to understand how the issues of power affected them so that they were unable to respond to the abuse in any assertive way.

Nelson, a fourteen-year-old, black young man was full of guilt that he had not responded aggressively and assertively to his swimming instructor who had sexually abused him. The abuse had occurred for six months when Nelson was twelve, and he had only disclosed when other children at the pool began to disclose their abuse by the same man. Nelson's older brother, aged fourteen at the time, was also propositioned by the abuser but had repelled him. This added to Nelson's feelings of guilt and his feeling that he was a coward. In a group of other abused children Nelson directed a scene where an adult (who was a co-therapist) played the swimming instructor and a small boy (who was about Nelson's height at twelve) played the child. Of course, the abuse was not re-enacted, only the preliminary grooming techniques of the swimming instructor. This psychodramatic mirroring of the scene helped Nelson to address issues of powerlessness. This same group also addressed issues of racial oppression, with black and white therapists working together, and so power and hierarchy were thoroughly explored.

Similarly, it is important for girls who have been abused to understand how males can oppress females. Patriarchy should be addressed with female children who have been sexually abused, especially with adolescents who are often beginning to recognise their own difficulties as young women.

The issue of gender as power must also be addressed when choosing a therapist for an abused child or for a therapeutic group. Many children, whether male or female, if they have been abused by a male, will feel safer with a female in the early days of therapy. Obviously those abused by a female will prefer a male worker. However, at a later stage in therapy it is often helpful for survivors to work in groups where there are co-therapists of both genders. They can see healthy interactions of male and female and they can practise relationships themselves with a safe adult.

CHILDREN WHO HAVE BEEN ABUSED IN ORGANISED RITUAL OR SATANIC GROUPS

I have chosen to discuss the survivors of ritual abuse in the chapter on 'difference' because I believe that such children invariably see themselves as different and because there are a number of considerations which make it important for workers to understand the especial sensitivities of these young people.

Most children in this situation will feel that all the power lies with the abusing group and that no outsiders can have any power. This is what they have been taught, often from a very early age. Most young children have some concept of the power of adults and some children rebel against it, as the mothers of many healthy two-year-olds know. The 'rebellion' against parents occurs again at five or six when teachers are seen as all-powerful. Later, of course, teachers face their own conflicts with children. Adolescents sometimes succeed in rebelling against all adults.

Children who have been abused within a group, however, are often drawn into the group when they are infants and they learn that they must obey the rules of the group. They are often encouraged to perform acts which make them uncomfortable, such as sexual acts with younger children or animals, and then this knowledge is used against them. They may also witness acts which appear to be illegal. Some children are convinced that they have seen babies killed although bodies have not been found. The power of the group as a whole, particularly if there is a charismatic leader, is stressed, and this is seen as omnipotent.

Therapy with such children is slow and has to be conducted with an understanding of the issues. It will be realised that children in this situation have not had a supportive ally whom they can tell about the abuse. In the first place their family or friendship networks may consist entirely of group members. When they go to school they are forbidden from attending extra-curricular activities or from bringing friends into their homes. Sometimes a child will talk to a teacher and this is the most common route for abuse to be discovered. As with Irene, whom we met in the chapter on children who abuse others, the abuse of children in groups may only be discovered when an adult or adolescent member of the group discloses. Occasionally, also, the behaviour of younger children is so bizarre that an investigation is started and the abuse discovered.

Children who have been abused in this way may choose to draw their feelings. Their drawings may be symbolic but may also contain disturbing features which are based in reality. A useful chapter on such drawings is by Mary Sue Moore in Valerie Sinason's book *Treating Survivors of Satanist Abuse* (1994). Moore mentions pictures of the devil and of dripping blood, pentagrams, and torn-off limbs, all of which appeared in Irene's drawings. Such pictures often raise strong feelings in the therapist and so a very supportive and understanding supervisor is required. I also feel strongly that a therapist for a ritually abused child should be 'contained' and supported within a team. A lone therapist will be unlikely to cope satisfactorily with the possible threats and emotional pressures.

Not surprisingly, when working with children who have been systematically and ritually tortured, the therapist often finds it difficult to concentrate and may have a sudden recall of a nauseous, humiliating or painful experience. It is important for the therapist to continue normally with the session, safe in the knowledge that she will be able to seek the support of a colleague immediately afterwards.

It is helpful to know something of the language and symbols which a ritually abused child may use. In Sinason's book (1994) Su Burrell gives a personal review of the literature. Predictably, many of the accounts are by adults and there is little on therapeutic work with children. It is useful to remember that some children who have been abused in this way are likely to use dissociation as a coping behaviour. This is not necessarily discouraged within the abusing group since children who are obviously dissociating, especially those who appear to have multiple personalities, can easily be dismissed by adults as 'mentally disturbed' and their statements treated as fantasies. As we have seen from Sinason's work, it may well be that some mental disability is a direct result of abuse.

Workers with abused children should always be alert to the possibility of ritualistic abuse, although most of us try not to recognise that it could ever occur. Social workers are often told to omit any details which might indicate this kind of abuse in criminal prosecution cases. This is because there is a great reluctance to accept evidence of satanic practice and it is easier to obtain a conviction on other evidence. This can inadvertently lead to further abuse of the child.

Ollie and Patrick were two brothers, aged seven and nine who, it was known, had been physically and sexually abused by their father and an uncle. Their mother had disappeared several years previously. On disclosure, by the younger boy to a teacher, the

boys had been removed from home and placed in a small child-
ren's home run by a religious order. At this time the nuns did not
wear a habit but the priest, who visited regularly, always wore his
cassock. The boys expressed great terror when they saw the priest
and refused to speak with him or to be in the same room. Both
boys became 'unmanageable' and their placement in the home was
threatened. In therapy they revealed that their abuse had taken
place within the context of a ritual wherein their father, uncle, and
several adult male friends had dressed as 'priests' and the boys, and
four other male cousins and friends, had undergone ceremonies of
mock sacrifice wherein their physical and sexual abuse had taken
place.

The therapy of children abused in ritualised or satanic groups is,
therefore, difficult. In my experience it takes several years, after
the child is removed from the abusive group, for healthy attachments to grow between the child and the foster parents. Once
these are in place then the therapy can begin. If healthy attachment has occurred then the foster parents have already demonstrated their understanding and patience and they may be relied
upon to support the child during therapy. It should be stressed,
however, that during therapy the child may revert to nightmares
or behaviour which had been painstakingly eliminated by the
foster parents. It is vital, therefore, that the carers are deeply
committed to the work in progress.

In the next chapter we look at the work which is necessary with
parents, carers and families whilst therapy with an abused child is
taking place.

8 PARENTS AND FAMILIES

> James James
> Morrison Morrison
> Weatherby George Dupree
> Took great
> Care of his Mother
> Though he was only three.
>
> A.A. Milne

So far, we have concentrated largely on individual work or groupwork directly with children. Of course, if we accept a model of child development which has an ecological structure, such as that of Bronfenbrenner, then we must accept that any changes which are effected in the child's behaviour will have repercussions in the family and even, possibly, in the wider community. We may accept, however, Virginia Axline's point in *Play Therapy* (1947), that a child who has successfully completed playtherapy may be strong enough to alter the behaviour of parents. She states that it is not always necessary for the parents to receive therapy because a child whose behaviour changes may become more acceptable to an adult. The adult, in turn, modifies his or her behaviour and a permanent change is achieved.

What she is noting is that any change of behaviour from one person in a family causes ripples which may have very far-reaching effects. This is the theory behind most types of family therapy. Family therapy has been used in conjunction with psychodrama for some time and several psychodramatists have written about it, notably Antony Williams (1989 and 1991). Most of the case examples given in the literature, however, do not apply to families with abused children. Many of the families who are referred for family therapy have suffered the loss of one parent, through divorce or death, some are having problems since a step-parent has joined. Yet others come to therapy because of the behaviour of a particular child who, it is discovered, is acting out marital problems which have not been discussed within the family.

Of course all these situations also occur in families where children have suffered abuse but in the more severe abuse cases (with which I have been involved) children are often in permanent foster care or have been placed for adoption. In these cases social workers have always been working with the new parents to help them to adapt to the change in their family.

The therapist with abused children may, therefore, be faced with several possibilities.

1. The child has been abused within the family but is remaining with them and the abuser or abusers are still at home.

2. The child has been abused within the family and the sole abuser has left home, leaving the child with one parent and, possibly, siblings.

3. The child has been abused (usually sexually) outside the family and the child is remaining at home.

4. The child has been abused (usually sexually) outside the family but has been removed from home. (This is usually because a child has been rejected by the family.)

5. The child has been abused within the family but has been removed from home. (This is usually because the abuser(s) refuse to leave home or the non-abusive parent minimises or denies the abuse.)

6. The child has been abused (and possibly neglected or abandoned) within the family and has been in foster care for some time and has now been released for adoption or for long-term fostering.

We may assume that a child is referred either because of behavioural difficulties or because of concern by parents or professionals that the child is not coping. It is vital, therefore, that the therapist assesses the situation thoroughly before deciding the best therapeutic options for that particular child and family. This preliminary assessment for management purposes may be done at an early stage, after reading the history and after discussion with any other professionals involved in the family. It may involve an initial meeting with the whole family, if this is appropriate, where options can be discussed with them and their motivation assessed.

After this assessment is made the therapist must consider each situation and decide how best to involve the parents or carers. Each family will have different needs, of course, but in this chapter we will look at some of the likely situations listed above and suggest how they could be managed.

1. Working with the whole family

Where the child has been abused within the home and continues to live at home with the abuser there may be a case for using psychodramatic techniques with the whole family. However, this is not advised with families where sexual abuse has occurred because of the difficulty of changing the balance of power, which usually rests very strongly with the abuser. The exception to this statement would be at a late stage in the procedure, after the child had received individual therapy and the abuser had received therapy or behaviour modification. Work would also have been done to help the non-abusing parent and, possibly, the siblings to cope. Couples therapy may also have been done and the final stage would consist of a few sessions with the whole family.

In a case like this, or in a less serious case where there had been physical abuse which was not life-threatening, a psychodramatist could ask the family to use physical enactments to show current family situations. It is important, though, not to ask families to show past abusive situations, for several reasons. Firstly, the problem is a technical one. In psychodrama the action can only show the perception of one person, the protagonist. The 'true picture' of any event, as we have seen, is impossible if all feelings and motivations are taken into account. If all the participants to an event are actually present there will be several different perceptions and it will become impossible to find one which is acceptable to everyone.

Secondly, the therapist usually asks the abuser(s) to make a contract that there will be no further abuse whilst the therapy is proceeding. If past abuse is re-enacted it may serve as a reminder to the abuser of the relief or pleasure they gained from the action. This could be a trigger for further abuse. In addition, of course, to re-enact an abusive scene with the actual abuser (even if it stopped short of the abusive act) may be too terrifying or confusing for the child.

However, enactments can be used to show current interactions, and also family members who have died or left, but who still have influence over the family, can be played, within the enactment by other family members in role reversal. This often helps families to realise the repeated patterns within families and the importance or significance of family rituals.

Family therapists often use genograms or family trees for the same purpose. By making a diagram of the family history, members can see the inevitability of some repeated actions. Showing the scene in action, however, adds an extra dimension.

The teachers at Ruth's school had reported suspicious bruising on her face and arms. On investigation Ruth's mother, Jane, had admitted that she had been slapping and punching her daughter. Ruth, aged nine, was Jane's first child, born when Jane was eighteen and unmarried. Jane was now happily married to Robert and they had two younger children, aged four and two. Jane said that Ruth had begun to irritate her beyond belief but she and the social workers had not uncovered the reason for Jane's uncharacteristic violence. No obvious pattern could be seen to explain Jane's actions although she accepted that Ruth herself was not to blame. The whole family agreed to attend for a therapy session in which they acted out typical scenes from their day. At one point Ruth hurled herself onto her stepfather's lap just as Jane entered the room, having put the younger children to bed. The therapist noticed the expression on Jane's face and stopped the action. 'What are you afraid of?' the therapist asked Jane. She began to cry. 'My stepfather', she said.

The therapist asked to see Jane alone or with Robert. Jane brought Robert to a session where she said that she had been sexually abused by her stepfather. The abuse had started when she was nine (Ruth's age) and had gone on for five years until Jane had gone to live voluntarily with her grandmother. She had told Robert about the abuse some years before because he had wondered why she did not visit her mother when her stepfather was around. Jane had never worked on her guilt feelings about the abuse. She had felt that she must have initiated it and this feeling was strengthened by her mother who waivered between disbelief and blaming the child. Mother's refusal to leave her husband also emphasised Jane's guilt.

Jane realised that she was fearful that Ruth would be sexually abused, although she did not really suspect Robert, who was quite different from her stepfather. Jane eventually joined a support group for adults abused as children and her physical abuse of Ruth was not repeated.

2. Working with the family where the abuser has left

This is a common situation, especially in severe physical abuse or in sexual abuse, where the mother leaves home, taking the children with her, to escape the violence. She herself may be a victim of domestic violence. Sometimes the abuser has left because he is in prison or in drug rehabilitation and no reconciliation is planned. In some instances sexual abuse may have been suspected but not confirmed and the abuser has simply disappeared and moved on.

In most of these cases a social worker will already be involved and an assessment may have been made of the remaining parent's ability to cope alone. This ability is seldom in doubt if a mother has taken the massive step of leaving an abusive man, taking her children with her. Sometimes, though, it is found that a mother has formed a series of partnerships with abusive men and that she seems to have great difficulty in coping alone.

Any therapy which is done with the children in such cases must be done in parallel with therapy for the mother. Because of issues of confidentiality and trust it is not helpful for the same therapist to see mother and child, or children, but there must be good communication between therapists because work with abused children will be very difficult if they are inappropriately supporting their mother. Even very young children can become 'parentified' and may protect their mothers to a degree which may put themselves at risk from abusers.

The therapist for the mother will have to work with the mother on her vulnerability, which may have originated in her own abuse, and also on her own parenting and protective skills. We know from research (Goodwin 1981) that sexually abused children who are not supported by their mothers are likely to suffer more damaging and long-term effects. For many years popular mythology supported the belief that mothers were to blame if children were abused by their fathers. This belief was also perpetuated by family systems therapists who appeared to collude with the 'diffusion of blame' for the abuse amongst all members of the family. Mothers, full of guilt feelings when their daughters revealed abuse, blamed themselves for unsatisfactory sexual relationships with their husband. Often the perpetrator would project this onto the mother who, only too eager to expiate some of the guilt, would inappropriately accept the blame. Unfortunately this often led to a collusion with the perpetrator who minimised and rationalised his own culpability. Specialists in work with offenders now know that the key to improvement with this client group is that they should take full responsibility for their actions.

Working with the mother then, often consists of enabling her to accept that the roots of her partner's crime almost invariably lie in his own early childhood experiences. She needs to understand that his abuse of a child or children is in addition to his failure to make satisfactory relationships with adults. It may be that both the mother and her husband have suffered childhood experiences that make relationships difficult. In this case, however, only the male parent has gone on to abuse a child.

It is likely too that the mother will feel guilty about her failure to protect her child or children. Providing her with information about how abusers carefully plan their assaults will help her to realise how she has been deliberately disempowered or circumvented by the abuser. As the therapist explains how abusers groom children to be abused, she may recall instances where this was happening, although she did not recognise it. This will help her to understand that the abuse was not an impulsive event but a series of progressive, planned events which culminated in the criminal behaviour.

It will be realised that this educative work is probably best done in a group situation, rather than with individuals. Indeed most mothers of sexually abused children, in this situation, will benefit from the support and encouragement of other women in a group. The lessening of isolation, the support and encouragement, are all powerful healers. As the mother is healed, so she can support and heal her child.

In order to build self-esteem with mothers in a group, the therapist may use role-training exercises to practise assertiveness. As in work with abused children, however, this stage of the work should not begin too soon. Educative work, providing information about abusers as described above, should take place first. As a mother remembers how subtly the 'grooming' of the child was achieved, and how she was deceived, some of her own guilt may be removed. Only then can her assertiveness be encouraged.

It will be at this stage that a mother's anger may be triggered. The anger, which may have been repressed for many years, can be encouraged and supported by other group members. The power of the anger, which is often feared by the women, can be contained within the group as a whole. It is important that the therapist should feel comfortable in working with anger.

Susie was a quiet young woman, in her twenties, with three little girls aged five, three and eighteen months. She was shattered when

*her eldest girl told a teacher at school about her father's long-term
sexual abuse of her. Later it was suspected that the three-year-old
had also been abused. Susie courageously left home with the children and was rehoused. She joined the group for mothers of sexually abused children because she was depressed and isolated and
her role in the group was usually as a support to others who were
more able to express their distress or anger. In a session, group
members had begun by complaining about 'officials' who withheld
benefit payments, then about social workers who missed appoint-
ments. Sensing a high energy level in the group, the therapist asked
each member to make a short statement expressing feelings about
'officials' and to illustrate it physically. To show their angry feelings
the group could either kick some large floor cushions, tear some
cardboard boxes, or hit the wall with a bataka or 'hitting stick'
made from rolled up newspaper, tightly taped. Susie looked doubt-
ful and at first kicked a cushion somewhat tentatively. Gradually
the movements of the whole group escalated and Susie became the
focus. She shouted all her pent-up feelings about her husband as
she banged the bataka onto the wall. She received great support
from the other women and she was then much more able to
participate in assertiveness exercises as she understood the difference between anger and assertiveness. Her depression lifted and
she was able more fully to support her three children.*

The therapist for the child, who is working in parallel with the
mother's therapist or group therapist, may need to teach the child
to relinquish some of the inappropriate responsibility and to play
in a childlike way. Sometimes this is simply a matter of introducing the child to appropriate materials and, of course, of giving the
child undivided attention for a whole hour each week.

Occasionally, when a mother has left home with her children
because of violence, one or more of the children can blame the
mother for the feelings of loss and grief which they are feeling.
They may be well aware of the abuse that all the members of the
family have suffered but they cannot make sense of the pain they
are feeling, which is like a bereavement. The mother may not need
therapy but may accept the support of a group. The child, however,
may be referred for therapy because his behaviour may be defiant
and rebellious or even violent to other children.

*Sean had moved from Ireland with his mother and sister to a town
in England where they hoped their physically abusive father would
not find them. Now aged twelve, Sean alternated between very*

protective behaviour towards his mother and very bullying behaviour towards his two younger sisters and to other children at school. He had come rather reluctantly for therapy after he had been suspended from school for a week. The therapist was finding it difficult to engage with Sean and, in desperation, had brought into the third session a small drum and a pipe (both from Ireland). As usual Sean ignored these, as he ignored the other equipment, and he gazed out of the window. The therapist tapped her fingers on the bodhran (Irish drum) and Sean turned round and picked up the pipe. 'I used to have one of these', he said. 'Can you play it?' invited the therapist. He nodded and played a few slow bars. Abruptly he put it back on the table. 'You look very sad', remarked the therapist. Sean nodded and gazed at the therapist mutely, his eyes full of misery. 'Sometimes we have to be angry because we are afraid of being too sad', she said.

From that point Sean was able to express his sadness about all he had lost and to understand that his anger with his mother was a defence against the pain of loss.

It is important, in a case like Sean's, that after he has received therapy, and his mother has received the support or therapy she requires, Sean and his mother, and any other children, come together to make sure that any misunderstandings are cleared up. Children sometimes need the support of their therapist in order to say difficult things to their mother. As long as mother has her own supporter this can be encouraged in a joint session.

3. Working with the family where a child has been abused outside

Where children are abused by strangers, by friends, or by relatives who do not live in the home, the parents usually feel deeply guilty and responsible. Each parent, however, will react very differently. It is extremely difficult for parents to support children when the parents themselves are struggling with their own fears and sense of loss. Some parents, particularly fathers, become extremely angry and although this is focused upon the abuser, this is not apparent to the child who feels that the parent's anger is directed at them. Some mothers feel so anxious and afraid that the child picks up these feelings, which are then impossible to resolve unless both mother and child can acknowledge them. Often a few explanatory sessions with the parents, to explain the dynamics of abuse, are all that is required. The parents are able to express their feelings and then they, in turn, can help the child to move on.

Tania's parents were both social workers and were horrified when they discovered that Tania had been sexually abused for twelve months when she was five, by a male cousin aged ten, who was staying in the house with his mother on a temporary basis. After the boy and his mother were rehoused Tania was able to tell her mother what had happened. The parents came together to see the therapist for two sessions and they were able to express their fears and anxieties, especially with regard to Tania's future. Tania loved drawing and they had noticed that while the cousin was in the house she had always drawn with a black pen and refused to use crayons, felt tips or paint. Consequently her drawings contained no colour. After the disclosure and Tania's outpouring of feelings to both parents, she began to use the coloured pens, which had always been available, and which she had used before the abuse, and she produced many colourful drawings.

It was not necessary, in this case, for Tania to have therapy since her parents were well able to support her, once they had received the support for themselves.

Not all families are as supportive of their child as Tania's. Some children may be abused outside the home because they are made more vulnerable by parental neglect or emotional abuse.

Thomas was one of several eleven- to thirteen-year-old boys who had been abused by a paedophile living nearby. The man used pornographic videos and computer games to attract the boys. Thomas's parents initially appeared supportive when therapy was suggested. Although a very bright child, his schoolwork was suffering and his teachers felt that he was depressed. After three assessment sessions with the therapist Thomas was keen for the work to continue. The therapist was worried however, at a review meeting with the parents, when they used the session to focus solely on their own problems, and totally ignored Thomas. Support for them was immediately set up with a social worker, but their behaviour at subsequent meetings remained the same. Separate therapy was then started, for each parent, when it became clear that Thomas could not progress because of the severe neglect and emotional abuse which he was experiencing from them.

One of the difficulties in working with parents in this way is that

the child is growing and developing, despite their abuse or neglect.
He or she is not receiving the attention necessary and which one
or two hours of therapy per week cannot supply. The younger the
child the more urgent is the need for changes in the parents. For
Thomas, help may have come too late to prevent damage. It is
ironic that further abuse by a paedophile was the trigger which
exposed his long-term abuse.

4. and 5. Working with a child who has been rejected by the family

Many of the children I have worked with have been completely
rejected by their families of origin. They have often been physically, sexually and emotionally abused for many years. Sometimes
the abuse has occurred entirely within the family and sometimes
part of the abuse has been perpetrated outside the family. Neglect
or emotional abuse may not be admitted and the child is seen as
causing or colluding in his or her own abuse. Such children,
already expressing disturbed behaviour, may be moved from one
foster home to another, as their behaviour escalates. Eventually
they may end up in 'secure accommodation' or, if they move on to
criminal offences, in prisons for young offenders.

Foster parents and professional carers have, traditionally,
received little training and sometimes do not get the support or
supervision they deserve. Their job is vitally important and
resources to assist in selection, training and support should be
found. Financially this would save millions in containing offending adolescents who have been let down by society in this way.
It has frequently been perceptive foster parents who have recognised the need for a child to receive therapy but it is sometimes
more difficult to persuade these carers to accept support for
themselves.

Part of the job of the therapist for the child is to communicate
with the foster parents to explain to them how the work is likely
to affect the child. To preserve confidentiality, and to reassure the
child about this, it may be best to do this in open meetings where
the young person is present. With a young child this may be
impractical and separate meetings may, therefore, be negotiated.
Carers can often describe areas which concern the child but which
the child has not been able to communicate with the therapist so
far. It is important, however, for the therapist to distinguish those
areas which concern the *carer or foster parent* rather than the

child. Sometimes such parents may have events from their own childhood which they are projecting onto the child. Being aware of this is sufficient for the child's therapist because it is rare that a child's own concerns will not be expressed in the therapy, when the child is ready. A simple explanation of this, to the foster parent, is helpful to allay fears that 'the real worries are not being dealt with'.

The carer's genuine worries about disruptive behaviour, however, must not be ignored by the therapist. Suggestions for controlling difficult behaviour, or support for sensible controls which the carer has initiated, should be given by the therapist. Foster parents often worry that they cannot ignore one child who is throwing food around the room because this will obviously affect any other children, as well as ruining their home. They fear that stopping this behaviour may be interpreted by the child (and possibly by the therapist) as punishing an already damaged child. They need to know that a child whose behaviour is out of control will feel more secure if firm rules are consistently applied. This does not preclude loving, supportive, listening sessions with the child after the behaviour has calmed down.

Professional carers in children's homes should receive regular supervision and training but often this is not forthcoming. Recent exposures in Britain of abusive behaviour by some carers in large children's homes, in the past, show how easy it is for an abusive culture to be encouraged where there is insufficient selection, training and support. Non-abusing carers then leave, because they suspect abuse or simply feel stressed by the abusive culture. Abusers in powerful positions then recruit more abusive staff and the dreadful situations are perpetuated.

Working with teams of staff of children's homes or special schools, where sexual abuse has been uncovered, can be a difficult but satisfying job for a psychodramatist who is prepared to work sociodramatically with the whole team. Where a sexual abuser or abusers have been removed there will remain many staff who feel guilty that they 'turned a blind eye'. Other staff will feel guilty at what they see is a 'witch hunt' against certain abusers whilst other abusive behaviour is ignored. It is possible for these feelings to be expressed, within the safety of a group session. In addition the team can be encouraged to show the hierarchies and links which developed in the group and how the abusive members encouraged secrecy. This work could be compared with the work done with a family where the abuser has left.

6. Working with adopters or long-term foster parents

The preparation of adopters or long-term foster parents to receive
abused children may not always be done thoroughly because of
fears that if the extent of the abuse, and the amount of difficult
behaviour, is revealed, then the child will become unplaceable.
Although this is understandable, it is not always helpful since the
new parents may then feel resentful about how unprepared they
were. Therapists are not usually involved in this preparation but
only become involved when the placement is threatened because of
disruptive behaviour by the child.

Therapy with the child is then put in place but too often the
new parents are neglected. They then may expect the child to be
'cured' and the problem solved. Obviously the therapist should
keep a close communication with these parents, in the same way
that we would with short-term foster parents or with natural
parents. In addition, the therapist should check how much information and education the new parents have been given about
abusive behaviour and its effects on the child. If this has not been
done there can be misunderstandings which can have dangerous
consequences for some children.

*Val had stayed with her mother after her father left home when
she was two. A stepfather joined the family when she was three
and when she was five she revealed how both parents had been
sexually abusing her and her younger siblings for some time. She
was now eleven and had been living with her adoptive family for
two years. Recently her schoolwork had deteriorated and mother
reported that she had become clingy and was refusing to attend
school. At first it was thought that Val was simply not settling in
the new school she had recently joined. Investigations into this,
and possible bullying, produced no result. Val had plenty of friends
who had moved up from primary school with her and she had
remained a popular girl and had made some new friends in addition. She did not appear to be having trouble with the academic
work and she herself had no explanation for school refusal other
than she 'didn't like it'. In therapy sessions it soon became clear
that Val was worried about leaving her mother because she was
insecure about losing her. Further work revealed her fears that 'dad
didn't like her anymore'.*

*Val agreed that the therapist could talk to her parents alone and
the problem soon surfaced. At eleven, Val was beginning to 'flirt'*

*with her father, in the way that many little girls do, secure in the
knowledge that dad will not react sexually. Val's behaviour may
have been more sexualised than some girls' because of her previous
experiences and Val's new dad became alarmed. He confessed that
he was feeling very confused by his own reactions and he had 'put
a stone wall up' and kept Val at a distance. Val, in turn, felt
rejected and could not understand how she had offended. The
therapist worked with both parents to help them to understand the
effects of Val's premature sexualisation, but also to help them realise that her current behaviour was within normal developmental
boundaries. Val's mother joined in several small role plays where
both parents showed the incidents which had caused problems.
They were then given strategies to cope with these and Val's
mother, in particular, was given support in helping her daughter to
deal with sexual situations with which she may be faced in future.*

It will be seen that there can be no formula for working with
parents and carers, just as there is no formula for working with
children. Antony Williams (1989) describes working with a whole
family where the father was enabled to show psychodramatically
how he had the fantasy of a 'perfect family' where his daughters
waited upon him in the manner of daughters of past generations.
Through enactment of the fantasy this father became aware of its
absurdity and of how he had been trying to force his daughters to
fulfil an unrealistic family pattern. As we saw with Ruth, in our
first example in this chapter, her mother Jane was unconsciously
expecting a family pattern to be repeated and, in re-enacting it, she
understood how unrealistic this was.

For some families this work together is helpful but for others it
is only possible to keep open lines of communication, and to give
careful explanations. Some parents secretly resent the intrusion of
a therapist, whom they see as usurping their role. It may be easier
for them to cast the therapist as a medical expert who is 'curing'
their child, rather than to see her as a colleague with whom they
can work to ensure that their child receives what she needs. Of
course, the therapist too may be guilty of taking on the 'cure-all'
role and of deliberately excluding the parent.

In child abuse it is only too easy for the therapist to adopt this
'rescuing' role. When the parents are the abusers this is, perhaps,
understandable, but it is not helpful. Where parents remain involved with the child, 'working in partnership' with them (to quote
the Children Act 1989) must remain a goal. This, however, is far
from easy where parents themselves have been proved to be

neglectful or abusive. A child therapist must always remain child centred, and keep the child's welfare at the forefront of therapy. She should also bear in mind, however, that healthy development depends on 'good-enough parenting' and if a child can receive this from one person in her family circle then this may be sufficient to mitigate the lack of it in a particular parent.

This is not, of course, to condone abuse of a child in any way. Subsequent abuse of a child, by a carer, which is revealed in the course of therapy, cannot be ignored. Our agreement with the child, and with the carers, at the planning stage, ensures that everyone understands that the therapist is not an investigator but may need to pass on information to those who are. If this occurs the 'partnership' with the parents disappears because the balance of power has immediately shifted from a shared position to one where the therapist has power. The co-operation between parents and therapist may be revealed to be superficial as the therapist takes control.

Even when no further abuse is revealed there may still be suspicion of the therapist by the parents. Their own guilt about known abuse may cause them to project this onto the therapist, whom they see as 'blaming them for everything'. They then may become defensive and seek to find other explanations for their child's behaviour. Anger is often expressed against the school or nursery, against social services or doctors and it takes skill and patience to work alongside such parents until they feel safe enough to discuss their own fears and doubts about their parenting.

One of the most difficult situations for a parent, or carer, is to discover that their child is sexually abusing others. As we saw in chapter 6 it is important that the child is not given negative messages by a carer which contradict the cognitive changes which are being encouraged by the child's therapist. It is fairly common for parents to collude with the child's denial, to blame the victim, or to minimise the abusive events. A straightforward, educative programme which enables parents to understand the dynamics of abuse is useful and is most effective if it is done in a group of parents whose children have exhibited abusive behaviour. Parents who understand that denial, victim blaming and minimising are part of an abuser's own coping mechanisms may realise how defensive their own reactions are and how unhelpful it is for their child.

Therapists for children can seldom work in isolation, therefore. They may need social workers, community workers, doctors and other therapists to work with the parents, and to work together for the benefit of the children. Research has now shown that even when children are separated from their parents it is important for links to be maintained (Dept of Health 1991). These contacts will affect the child's therapy. The therapist is unlikely to have any direct contact with parents who are separated from their children so contact with the agency (usually the Social Services) may be important. Parents, even absent parents, can either help to move the therapy on or can block it.

Parents need to be motivated in order to co-operate and motivation can come from an understanding that they are sharing the power with the therapist. There will be little likelihood of co-operation with parents who feel disempowered by the therapist. Feelings of disempowerment can be exacerbated where there are differences of class or of race and culture between therapist and parents. Respecting these differences, especially with regard to differing parenting practices, can help co-operation to flourish.

Finally, the therapist may need to assist parents, foster parents and adoptive parents to believe in their child's capacity to heal. Years ago, popular Western culture held that children do not remember early abuse and are not affected by total separation and loss. Evidence over the last forty years has shown that memory does not act like a video tape; seldom do we have total recall of our childhoods. Nevertheless, fragments of memory are retained from our very early experience. Pre-verbal events are 'remembered' as feelings, bodily sensations, or unexplained reactions and all these affect our current functioning. Often, through play, and through the love and care of others, we can resolve some of the confusion and pain which results from early trauma.

Psychodrama, dramatherapy and playtherapy use the inherent capacity of the child, together with the skills of the therapist, to 'sort out the muddles' and enable the child to function more comfortably. During the last decade, when the damaging effects of abuse have been fully realised, popular beliefs have moved to another extreme position, believing that those who have been seriously abused cannot recover; or that they will need years of therapy before they can function adequately.

Of course, some adults may need a long time, and possibly much therapeutic help, before they feel that they have truly survived their experiences. Children, however, usually start to recover much more quickly. Between ten and twenty sessions are usually enough for most abused children (although they may return for more work as they develop). Some older children who have suffered multiple abuse may need longer, up to forty sessions.

A child's developmental stage should always be taken into

account, however. Some adolescent behaviours, whilst irritating to a parent, are completely functional as they serve to separate the child from the parent and to encourage individuality and independence. Some parents mistake this 'normal' behaviour for dysfunctional behaviour which reflects the abuse the child has suffered. Perhaps this can best be illustrated in the words of the wise foster parent of an adolescent, Wendy, with whom I had been working for six months:

'Wendy's definitely much better now. She's started being "bolshie", you know, like teenagers do. I don't like it, no parent would, but I know it's normal, so she must have got her confidence back.'

This is the kind of subjective response, from parents and children, which helps us to evaluate the therapy we do with young people. In our final chapter we will look at the attempts which have been made to evaluate treatment more objectively.

9   DOES IT WORK?

'Dreams is very mystical things,' the BFG said. 'Human beans
is not understanding them at all. Not even their brainiest
prossefors is understanding them.'

                              from *The BFG* by Roald Dahl

How can we know whether child psychotherapy is working? What
criteria can we use to judge whether children are recovering from
traumatic abuse? Measuring therapeutic progress is difficult in any
circumstances. Researchers into therapeutic outcome usually ask
clients for their opinion on their own progress, or they are asked to
complete psychological tests at the beginning and end of therapy.
Even the latter are somewhat subjective. The therapist is also
usually asked for an opinion of the client's progress and this, too,
may be difficult to measure. If the therapist is inexperienced how
can she judge success if she has only seen a small number of
clients? If the therapy is client centred how can a therapist disagree
with the client's own assessment of the outcome?

These questions must be answered by a serious researcher into
evaluation of therapy. With children the questions become even
more complex. Until fairly recently, within the last decade, it has
been almost unheard of to ask younger children, at least, for their
opinion on their therapeutic progress. This was probably based on
a mistaken feeling that children would not understand or be able
to give an opinion. It is probable too that this was a protective, as
well as a patronising attitude, and it grew out of attempts to
provide distractions, rather than therapy for children. As little as
ten years ago some childcare professionals were still recommending
that children should be encouraged to 'forget the traumatic events'.

In reality children who are regularly asked to assess their own
progress in therapy can provide us with much helpful information.
In addition, of course, parents and carers can also tell us about
changes in behaviour which may be indicators of progress.
Researchers must, however, be aware that changes in a child's

behaviour may not always be seen as positive by some carers. More autonomy and independence may be seen negatively by an over-protective parent. Very controlling parents sometimes see the whole therapeutic experience as intrusive and unnecessary for their child. They may have felt pressured to comply, especially if their child has been abusing others or participating in criminal activity, and they are reluctant to admit success.

EVALUATING THE TREATMENT OF CHILDREN WHO ABUSE OTHERS

In an evaluative study of the therapy of children who were abusing others (Bannister & Gallagher 1995) one parent was critical that the therapist allowed the child to decide what he was doing in the sessions and complained that the therapist was 'not pushy enough'. It may be, of course, that this young person would have benefited from a more confronting attitude from the therapist. As we have seen, children who abuse usually need a dual programme which works on the abusive behaviour, as well as on the child's victim experiences. It may also be that the parent was not well informed about the methods used in the therapy or that the child chose to stress only the more enjoyable aspects of his therapy. Whatever the reason, researchers must always be aware of the subjectivity of parental responses and of their own subjectivity in drawing conclusions from these.

With children who abuse, or commit criminal acts, the amount of recidivism may be a good measure of the success of the therapeutic programme. In a study of adolescent offenders (Davis & Leitenberg 1987) the authors suggest that although about half of adolescent sexual offenders go on to commit further sexual offences, only about 10% do so after treatment. Most studies of adolescent sexual abusers conclude that complete programmes, using eclectic methods focused on this particular client group are the most successful treatment for young people who are abusing (for example see Thomas & Rogers 1983 and Kahn & Chambers 1991).

Most young people who are abusing others will not have received any therapy at all during their early years when they were probably being abused either emotionally, physically or sexually. Therapy after offences have been committed may be 'bolting the stable door after the horse has fled'. At least, however, these young people do receive the attention which was denied to them previously.

EVALUATING THE TREATMENT OF CHILD SURVIVORS OF ABUSE

It is clear that suffering abuse, especially over long periods or in conjunction with other stressors, may interfere with normal child development. Studies of the most effective methods of treatment must, therefore, continue. Bagley & King (1990) remind us of the almost certain causal link between childhood sexual abuse and later mental health problems. They recommend individual therapy for victims as a first priority, followed later by self-help groups for survivors.

My own experience suggests that individual therapy for child victims should definitely be a priority because if intervention comes later the treatment takes much longer and the outcome is less clear. Most abused adults, who are still suffering many years after the trauma, will need not only extensive personal therapy but also group therapy or support.

Dempster & Roberts (1991), well-known practitioners and researchers in Scotland, also agree with this priority and their paper underlines the difficulties in trying to evaluate treatment methods. Their own attempts to evaluate their treatment programme in Dundee were fraught with problems, not least the fact that several children in the control group of 'unabused children' later revealed that they had been sexually abused.

In 1992 O'Donohue & Elliot published a paper describing eleven treatment evaluations for sexually abused children. They found methodological problems with all of them. Some described single cases only. The authors demanded more research and pointed out that this should look specifically at which kind of treatment suited a specific child. They realised, even from these flawed studies, that the most successful outcome was likely to be where the therapist was flexible and creative enough to tailor the treatment for each child.

Other practitioners (Robert Wheeler & Lucy Berliner 1988) have also suggested that eclectic treatment methods are likely to be necessary, according to the particular problem of each child. Most writers on treatment of younger children (as opposed to adolescents) stress the importance of also working with the child's mother or carer. For older children, however, it may be possible to work solely with the young person if parents are not very co-operative.

EVALUATING THE RELATIONSHIP BETWEEN THERAPIST AND CHILD

Suzanne Long (1986) writing in the early days of treatment of young sexually abused children, declares that the basic attitudes of the therapist are important. She describes these as 'Respect, acceptance and faith'. I would subscribe to her view that the therapist must respect the child for her feelings at that moment, and not try to take these feelings away. Acceptance of the child goes along with this and faith is Long's word to describe the belief that the child can heal herself. If we work within these principles, then I feel that some benefit and healing must accrue to the child.

Rogers (1951), of course, stresses that the attitude and orientation of the counsellor to the client is all-important. He quotes research to support his belief that understanding and acceptance are crucial. He states that this acceptance of the client's world is even more important when working with children because it may be that the counsellor does not fully 'understand' so may have to accept blindly. I believe it was Yalom who also stated that his study of therapeutic outcome led him to the opinion that the client–therapist relationship was much more important than any other factor.

EVALUATING THE CHILD'S RESPONSE TO THERAPY

In my own work children are always asked about their feelings regarding the therapy, at frequent intervals. At the first meeting their motivation is assessed. A child may describe her wish to enter therapy as a need to 'behave better so mum doesn't get cross'. I explain that the purpose of therapy is to help her to feel better about herself. If she behaves differently after therapy and mother likes the new behaviour then that is all to the good. The point, however, is to make the child, not the mother, feel better.

After about six sessions I ask the child which parts of the therapy they enjoyed or found helpful and if there is anything they were not happy with. We discuss this and also share ideas on how the child's behaviour may have changed. Of course with younger children this kind of discussion is very brief and may consist of quick reminders about parts of the therapy (looking at pictures painted for instance), with the child expressing feelings about them. Then we have a meeting with parent or carer and, perhaps, the social worker or other referrer. The evaluation continues at this meeting with the adults giving their evaluative opinions and their expectations or hopes for future work.

Although the adults' opinions are always taken into account, the decisions about continuing or finishing therapy are always made by the therapist, on a clinical basis, after discussion with the child wherever possible. Occasionally, of course, children will be removed prematurely from therapy, for a variety of reasons, and the therapist has to cope with the anger or loss or confusion which she herself feels.

The child's feelings about the sessions are again sought at frequent intervals throughout the therapy and I believe that this consultation helps children to consolidate their feelings of success or improvement. Anne Peake (1996), describing a therapeutic group for boys all abused by the same paedophile, used a simple questionnaire with such questions as 'How do you feel now about what happened to you?' This was administered after finishing the group and was evidently completed even by the youngest boys who were eight years old. She concluded that all the boys could talk more easily about their experiences and they all now shared this with their mothers. If a therapeutic group can provide a forum for witnessing a child's story and can enable that child to seek support from a parent, then it must have performed a very helpful function.

EVALUATING THE SPECIFIC BENEFITS OF PSYCHODRAMA, DRAMATHERAPY AND OTHER CREATIVE THERAPIES, WITH ABUSED CHILDREN

An outcome which is frequently noted in children who have received an eclectic, creative approach to therapy, is the increase in their own ability for creative expression. In non-directive play children will choose the medium which has most impact for them at the time. It is important that different media are always available since the child's needs will change over time. A young child may be developing naturally from embodied play, through projective play to role play. An older child whose development has been delayed, perhaps because of the abuse, may progress rapidly through these stages and the therapist must, therefore, be alert to changing needs.

In addition, a child may move from conscious thoughts about the abuse to unconscious and pre-verbal feelings. These are 'remembered' as a series of impressions, perhaps as feelings in response to images. It is unlikely that a child can make verbal statements about these memories. Nor is this absolutely necessary; their exploration through metaphor and image is sufficient for both child and therapist to understand and accept.

Will, aged twelve, abandoned by his mother in the hospital where he was born, was reunited with her at three months and then suffered multiple abuse from her and several father substitutes. This child, in the Special Needs class at school, moved classically through embodiment, projective and role play, in his therapeutic sessions. His swirling paintings with large splodges of violent colour dominated the first three months of his therapy. In discussions with the therapist he stated that the paintings expressed 'his feelings about what happened'. He was not, at this stage, able to verbalise his feelings in any way. Next he started writing songs, and singing them in the sessions, stating that they were for his mother or his stepfather. The songs projected feelings of loss, anger and pain onto these parental figures. He said that he thought they would be having these feelings now. Occasionally too, in this middle period, he used puppets or hero and monster figures to express feelings which he could not yet own. After six months he felt able to replay some of his own situations. At first, although Will was able to play all the roles, his scenes were totally in metaphor, using scenes from classical fairy stories. Later he was able to enact real situations. Will's main difficulty, before referral for therapy, had been extremely low self-esteem and worries about self-mutilation or self-destruction. On completion of therapy his self-assessment was high, his schoolwork had improved and his carers were delighted with his progress. As a self-confident adolescent he became much in demand at school for his obvious creative talents.

Of course, any psychotherapy must always be an ongoing possibility. It is unrealistic to state that a child can recover from all aspects of a severely abusive childhood after a few months of therapy. As the young person develops there may be fresh memories of abuse, or feelings may develop in response to circumstances. Not only will a child face the usual developmental crises of puberty and adolescence, of falling in love, and of the break up of relationships, but may also have specific life events which rekindle difficult feelings. When a parent dies (even if this is an abusing parent) there may be a return to recrimination and despair, a growth of further guilt and pain, even though these had been expressed at some point in therapy. When adults divorce or suffer the loss of a partner there may be a return to feelings of abandonment. A person who has received therapy in childhood will probably find it much easier to understand and cope with these bewildering feelings, either with the help of friends or professionals.

Yvonne was fifteen when she first came to therapy. She had told her mother and stepfather about the sexual abuse committed by her father, who had been abusing her on contact visits for about seven years. Her parents had found it difficult to understand Yvonne's involvement with drug-misusing friends and with much older 'boyfriends'. Therapy was difficult because Yvonne was torn between loyalty to her 'friends', her own abuse of and need for drugs, and her desire to recover from what her father had done to her. After three months therapy was terminated when Yvonne disappeared from home. She was found some months later, having been further raped and abandoned by her friends. Eventually she commenced a drug rehabilitation programme where psychodrama and dramatherapy were both used. She recovered rapidly and found it easy to utilise these therapeutic modes to which she was already accustomed. When she was seventeen she recommenced her studies and at eighteen she had published a small book of poems and was involved in writing a play.

J.L. Moreno wanted to be remembered as the man who brought joy and laughter into psychiatry. He is also frequently remembered as someone who saw the potential for his kind of drama with children when he worked and played with them in Vienna as a philosophy student. There is no doubt that he intended psychodrama to be used with children as well as adults. He and his wife Zerka have even described psychodramatic interventions with their son Jonathan. Psychodrama is used not only for 'sick' children but for all children to aid their emotional growth, to widen their role repertoire and to help them to empathise with others.

When Peter Slade used play, drama and dance with children he was convinced that it would aid their development. Eventually, through this, dramatherapy was evolved as an aid to solve problems as well as enhance development in children. Playtherapy began, as we have seen, as a specific way to use Carl Rogers' ideas on non-directive or client centred therapy, with children.

Despite this there is still some reluctance to introduce young children to drama in schools and nurseries. 'Acting out' is often described disparagingly by parents, teachers and health professionals.

'Acting out' is behaviour which may occur when children (and some-times adults) are not heard, when they cannot understand current events, when they are confused about feelings. Sometimes the acting out brings about self-healing but more often the behaviour has caused further problems because it is socially disruptive. 'Acting in' is a way of accepting behaviour which may otherwise be acted out. The behaviour is expressed in many different ways within the therapy so that the child can fully experience her own confusion and can begin to make sense of it. It is a way of unravelling the tangle and of knitting it up into a serviceable garment.

If drama, remedial drama, and play were more widely taught in teacher training and in parenting classes, then children could be encouraged to cultivate their own natural sources of healing and renewal. Children with communication difficulties could be shown how to communicate through creative expression, and adults could be taught to be more open about understanding this.

Moreno stated that a truly therapeutic procedure can have no less an objective than the whole of mankind. Mankind must include men and women of all cultures but, most of all, it must include all children. Drama has been used in many cultures, in the form of ritual, often for healing purposes, for centuries, even perhaps for thousands of years. Europe, Africa, Asia, all have claimed to be the cradle of drama. The drama of life begins in the cradle. If we nurture dramatic and creative expression in children it can nurture us throughout our lives.

REFERENCES

Abel, G.G., Becker, J.B. & Mittelman, M. (1985) Sex Offenders: Results of Assessment and Recommendations for Treatment, in H. Ben-Aaron, S. Hucker & C. Webster (eds) *Clinical Criminology: Current Concepts*, Toronto: M & M Graphics.

American Psychiatric Association (1994) *Diagnostic and Statistical Manual of Mental Disorders (DSM–IV)*, Washington, DC: American Psychiatric Press.

Axline, Virginia M. (1947 Orig.) (1969 Reprint) *Play Therapy*, New York: Ballantine Books.

Axline, Virginia M. (1964) *Dibs: In Search of Self*, London: Penguin Books.

Bagley, C. & King, K. (1990) *Child Sexual Abuse: the Search for Healing*, London: Routledge/Tavistock.

Bannister, Anne (1992) *From Hearing to Healing – Working With The Aftermath of Child Sexual Abuse*, Harlow, Essex: Longman.

Bannister, Anne (1995) Images & Action – Dramatherapy & Psychodrama with Sexually Abused Adolescents, in Jennings, Sue (ed.) *Dramatherapy with Children and Adolescents*, London: Routledge.

Bannister, A. & Gallagher, E. (1995) *Children Who Sexually Abuse Other Children*, Manchester: NSPCC.

Bannister,A. & Gallagher, E. (1997) Children Who Sexually Abuse Other Children, in Bates, J., Pugh, R. & Thompson, N. (eds) *Protecting Children: Challenges and Change*, Aldershot: Arena.

Bettelheim, Bruno (1976) *The Uses of Enchantment*, London: Penguin 1991.

Biblow, Ephraim (1973) in Singer, J.L. *The Child's World of Make-Believe*, New York: Academic Press.

Blatner, Adam and Blatner, Allee (1988) *The Art of Play*, New York: Human Sciences Press Inc.

Bowlby, J. (1951) *Maternal Care & Mental Health*, Geneva: WHO, London: HMSO, New York: Columbia University Press.

Bowlby, J. (1953) *Child Care and the Growth of Love*, Harmondsworth: Pelican Books.

Bowlby, J. (1969) *Attachment and Loss*, Vol. 1. London: Tavistock (Second Edition), Harmondsworth: Pelican (1984).

Bronfenbrenner, U. (1979) *The Ecology of Human Development*, Cambridge, Mass.: Harvard University Press.

Burrell, S. (1994) A personal review of the literature, in Sinason, V. (ed.) *Treating Survivors of Satanist Abuse*, London & New York: Routledge.

Carter, Angela (ed.) (1990) *The Virago Book of Fairy Tales*, London: Virago Press Ltd.

Cattanach, Ann (1992) *Play Therapy with Abused Children*, London: Jessica Kingsley Publishers.

Davis, C. & Leitenberg, H. (1987) Adolescent Sex Offenders, *Psychological Bulletin*, 101: 417–27.

Debelle, G.D., Ward, M.R., Burnham, J.B., Jamieson, R. & Ginty, M. (1993) Evaluation of Intervention Programmes for Juvenile Sex Offenders: Questions & Dilemmas, *Child Abuse Review*, Vol. 2, 75–87.

Dempster, H. & Roberts, J. (1991) Child Sexual Abuse Research: a methodological quagmire, *Child Abuse & Neglect*, 15: 593–5.

Department of Health (1991) *Patterns and Outcomes in Child Placement*, London: HMSO.

Dingwall, Robert (1989) Labelling Children as Abused or Neglected, in Stainton Rogers, W., Hevey, D. & Ash, E. (eds) *Child Abuse & Neglect: Facing The Challenge*, London: Batsford, for Open University.

Erikson, E. (1977) *Childhood and Society*, London: Paladin Books.

Fahlberg, Vera (1981) *Attachment and Separation*, UK: British Agencies for Adoption and Fostering.

Finkelhor, David (1984) *Child Sexual Abuse: New Theory & Research*, New York: Free Press.

Finkelhor, D. & Browne, A. (1985) The Traumatic Impact of Child Sexual Abuse and Conceptualisation, *American Journal of Orthopsychiatry*, Vol. 55 (4).

Fox, Jonathan (1987) *The Essential Moreno*, New York: Springer.

Freeman-Longo, R.E. (1982) Sexual Learning and Experience Among Adolescent Sexual Offenders, *International Journal of Offender Therapy and Comparative Criminology*, Vol. 26 (2): 235–41.

Gersie, Alida (1992) *Earthtales*, London: Greenprint (Merlin Press).

Gessell, Arnold (1971) *First Five Years of Life: A Guide to the Study of the Pre-school Child*, London: Methuen.

Gessell, Arnold et al. (1977) *The Child From Five to Ten*, New York, London: Harper & Row.

Gil, Eliana and Johnson, Toni Cavanagh (1993) *Sexualised Children*, Rockville, Md.: Launch Press.

Goodwin, J. (1981) Suicide attempts in Sexual Abuse Victims and their Mothers, *Child Abuse and Neglect*, 5: 217–21.

Hartman, C. & Burgess, A.W. (1988) Summary of Information Processing of Trauma, *Journal of Interpersonal Violence*, Vol. 3 (4).

Holmes, Paul (1992) *The Inner World Outside*, London: Tavistock/ Routledge.

Jennings, Sue (1987) *Dramatherapy – Theory & Practice for Clinicians & Teachers*, Beckenham, Kent: Croom Helm.

Jennings, Sue (1995) *Dramatherapy with Children and Adolescents*, London: Routledge.

Johnson, Toni Cavanagh (1988) Child Perpetrators – Children Who Molest Other Children, Preliminary Findings, *Child Abuse & Neglect*, 12: 219–29.

Kahn, T. & Chambers, H. (1991) Assessing Reoffense Risk with Juvenile Sexual Offenders, *Child Welfare*, 70: 333–45.

Kempe, R.S. and Kempe, C.H., (1978) *Child Abuse*, London: Fontana/Open Books.

Kennedy, M. (1996) Sexual Abuse and Disabled Children, in Morris, J. (ed.) *Encounters with Strangers: Feminism and Disability*, London: Women's Press.

Klein, M. (1975) *Collected Works, Vol. 1, Love, Guilt and Reparation*, London: Hogarth Press.

Lahad, Mooli (1992) Story Making in Assessment Method for Coping With Stress, in Sue Jennings (ed.) *Dramatherapy: Theory and Practice 2*, London: Routledge.

Lane, Sandy (1991) The Sexual Abuse Cycle, in Ryan, Gail D. and Lane, Sandy L. *Juvenile Sexual Offending: Causes, Consequences & Correction*, Lexington, Mass.: Lexington Books.

LaPorta, Lauren D. (1992) Childhood Trauma & Multiple Personality Disorder: The case of a nine-year-old girl, *Child Abuse & Neglect*, 16: 615–20.

Lindon, Jennie (1993) *Child Development From Birth to Eight*, London: National Children's Bureau.

Long, Suzanne (1986) Guidelines for Treating Young Children, in MacFarlane K., & Waterman, J. et al. (eds) *Sexual Abuse of Young Children*, London & Sydney: Holt, Rinehart and Winston.

Lowenfeld, M. (1979) *The World Technique*, London: George Allen and Unwin.

MacFarlane, Kee (1991) *When Children Molest Children*, Orwell Vt.: The Safer Society Press.

McElroy, L.P. (1992) Early Indicators of Pathological Dissociation in Sexually Abused Children, *Child Abuse & Neglect*, 16: 833–46.

Marineau, Rene F. (1989) *Jacob Levy Moreno 1889–1974*, London: Routledge.

Miller, Alice (1987a) *For Your Own Good*, London: Virago Press.

Miller, Alice (1987b) *The Drama of Being a Child*, London: Virago Press.

Miller, Alice (1990) *Banished Knowledge – Facing Childhood Injuries*, London: Virago Press.

Moore, M.S. (1994) Common Characteristics in the Drawings of Ritually Abused Children and Adults, in Sinason, V. (ed.) *Treating Survivors of Satanist Abuse*, London and New York: Routledge.

Moreno, J.L. (1965) *The Voice of J.L. Moreno*, a taped interview. Available from Holwell Centre for Psychodrama & Sociodrama, East Down, Barnstaple, Devon.

Moreno, J.L. (1977) *Psychodrama*, First Volume, 4th Edition, Beacon, N.Y.: Beacon House Inc.

NSPCC/Chailey Heritage/Dept of Health (1997) *Turning Points: A Resource Pack for Communicating with Children*, Leicester, NSPCC Training Dept.

O'Donohue, W.T. & Elliot, A.N. (1992) Treatment of the Sexually Abused Child: a Review, *Journal of Clinical Child Psychology*, 21: 218–28.

Peake, Anne (1996) Help for Children & Their Families, in Bibby, P.C. (ed.) *Organised Abuse*, Aldershot, Hants. & Brookfield, Vt.: Arena: Ashgate Publishing.

Pearson, J. (1996) *Discovering the Self through Drama and Movement*, London: Jessica Kingsley Publishers.

Piaget, Jean (1947) (Eng. trans. 1950) *The Psychology Of Intelligence*, London: Routledge & New York: Harcourt Brace.

Pierce, L.H. and Pierce, R.L. (1984) Race as a Factor in the Sexual Abuse of Children, *Social Work Research & Abstracts*, Vol. 20 (2): 9–14.

Rogers, Carl R. (1951) *Client Centred Therapy*, London: Constable & Co.

Rouf, Khadj (1990) My self in echoes. My voice in song, in Bannister, A. et al. (eds) *Listening to Children*, London: Longman.

Rutter, M. (1981) *Maternal Deprivation Reassessed* (2nd Edition), Harmondsworth: Penguin Books.

Ryan, Gail (1991) The System's Response to Juvenile Sex Offenders, in Ryan, Gail D. and Lane, Sandy L., *Juvenile Sexual*

Offending: Causes, Consequences & Correction, Lexington Mass.: Lexington Books.

Salter, A.C. (1988) *Treating Child Sex Offenders and Victims: a Practical Guide,* Beverley Hills: Sage.

Sgroi, Suzanne M. (1988) *Vulnerable Populations, Vol. 1,* Lexington Mass.: Lexington Books.

Sheridan, Mary (1973) *Children's Developmental Progress from Birth to Five: The Stycar Sequences,* London: NFER.

Siddall, R. (1994) The Hidden Taboo, *Community Care No. 1023,* 30 June p.11 'Inside' supplement.

Sinason, V. (1988) Smiling, Swallowing, Sickening and Stupefying: The Effect of Sexual Abuse on the Child, *Psychoanalytic Psychotherapy,* Vol. 3 (2): 97–111.

Slade, Peter (1995) *Child Play – Its Importance For Human Development,* London: Jessica Kingsley Publishers.

Smith, Peter K. and Cowie, Helen (1988) *Understanding Children's Development,* Oxford: Blackwell.

Spring, J. (1987) *Cry Hard & Swim: The story of an incest survivor,* London: Virago.

Sullivan, P.M. (1993) Sexual Abuse Therapy for Special Children, *Journal of Child Sexual Abuse,* Vol. 2 (2): 117–25.

Sullivan, P.M. and Scanlan, J.M. (1987) Therapeutic issues, in Garbarino, J., Brookhauser, P.E. & Authier, K.J. (eds) *Special Children – Special Risks: The Maltreatment of Children with Disabilities,* New York: De Gruyter.

Summit, R.C. (1983) The Child Sexual Abuse Accommodation Syndrome, *Child Abuse and Neglect,* 7: 177–93.

Thomas, J.N. & Rogers, C.M. (1983) A Treatment Program for Intrafamily Juvenile Sexual Offenders, in Geer, J.G. & Stuart, I.R. (eds) *The Sexual Aggressor: Current Perspectives on treatment,* New York: Van Nostrand Reinhold.

Vygotsky L. (1934 Orig.) (1961 R) *Thought and Language,* Cambridge, Mass.: MIT Press.

Warner, Marina (1994) *From The Beast to The Blonde,* London: Chatto & Windus Ltd.

Westcott, H. & Cross, M. (1996) *This Far and No Further: Towards Ending the Abuse of Disabled Children,* Birmingham: Venture Press.

Wheeler, J.R. & Berliner, L. (1988) Treating the Effects of Sexual Abuse on Children, in Wyatt, G.E. & Powell, G.J. (eds) *Lasting Effects of Child Sexual Abuse,* California: Sage Publishers.

Williams, A. (1989) *The Passionate Technique,* London & New York: Routledge.

Williams, A. (1991) *Forbidden Agendas*, London & New York: Routledge.

Winnicott, D.W. (1964) *The Child, the Family, and the Outside World*, Harmondsworth: Penguin Books.

Winnicot, D.W. (1971 & 1974) *Playing and Reality*, London: Tavistock; Harmondsworth, Pelican.

Wyatt, Gail Elizabeth and Powell, Gloria Johnston (eds) (1988) *Lasting Effects of Child Sexual Abuse*, Beverley Hills & London: Sage Publishers.

INDEX

Abel, G.G., 95
Aberfan disaster, 61
abuse
  acceptance of, 119–20
  and coercion, 105–6
  denial, 39
  disclosure, 50–1
  emotional, 137–8
  of power, 41
  PTSD model for understand-
    ing, 42–54
  recovery from, 143–4, 150–1
  reporting, 72–3
  ritual, 103–4, 126–8
  theories of, 40–1, 145–6
  traumagenic dynamics model
    for understanding, 54–7
  use of dissociation to cope
    with, 32–4, 46–7
  within family, 130–6, 138–9
  see also coping mechanisms;
    sexual abuse; trauma;
    treatment
abusers
  adolescent sexual, 95–6
  adult sexual, 92–5
  behaviour of, 46, 58
  cognitive distortions, 51–2
  professional carers as, 139
  and stigmatisation, 55–6
  use of coercion, 105–6
  see also adolescents; adults;
    children who abuse; sexual
    abuse

adolescents
  coping mechanisms, 32
  recidivism among, 146
  use of stories for, 76–7
  see also children who abuse
adoptive parents, working with,
  140–1
adults
  children's expectations of,
    58
  controlling behaviour of, 59
  coping mechanisms, 31
  as sexual abusers, 92–5, 100
anal penetration, 105
assessment
  of adolescent abusers, 97–9
  of therapeutic needs, 18–19,
    34–8
attachment and bonding,
  27–31, 37
  after abuse, 128
autism, 122
Axline, Virginia, 16, 129
  playtherapy, 8

Bagley, C., and K. King, 147
Battered Baby Syndrome
  (Kempe), 40
'battle fatigue', 43
betrayal, 56
Bettelheim, Bruno, and fairy
  stories, 79, 80, 82
Blatner, Adam, theory of child
  development, 5

Index by Auriol Griffith-Jones